Contents

Introduction   v

**Oxford A–Z of Grammar   1
and Punctuation**

D0052087

Introduction

How English sentences work

This reference book is organized so that readers can find the terms they are looking for as quickly as possible. For this purpose an A–Z arrangement is the most suitable. The problem with grammar, however, is that in order to understand one term, you usually need to know what one or more other terms mean. For example, if you look up the term ABSTRACT NOUN the explanation assumes that you know what a NOUN is. If you look up NOUN, it takes it for granted that you know what a PHRASE is, and so on. Readers who have little or no background knowledge about grammar may find this very frustrating. So the purpose of this brief introduction is to explain the basic terms of English grammar.

Sentences

Grammar is a way of describing how words are combined to form sentences.

Each of the words in that sentence can be used in particular ways to form sentences. So each can be allocated to a WORD CLASS (or 'part of speech'):

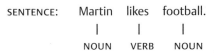

Parts of a sentence

Putting words into classes like this tells us a lot about how words are used, but it doesn't tell us much about how sentences are constructed. To do that we need to look at sentences in a different way. We do this by looking for patterns in the way that sentences are constructed. For example, we can see that these two sentences follow a similar pattern:

Martin	likes	football.
Mary	writes	books.

If we think a bit, we can see that the sentence below follows a similar pattern, even though it is longer:

Our friends at number 29 are going to visit their relatives in Australia.

We can see this more clearly if we set the sentences out in a table:

A	B	C
Martin	likes	football.
Mary	writes	books.
Our friends at number 29	are visiting	their relatives in Australia.

The first thing to notice is that each cell in the table can contain one word (e.g. *likes*) or a group of words (e.g. *are visiting*). But each cell contains a word or words that have a particular job to do in the sentence. The first cell tells us what the sentence is going to be about; it contains the SUBJECT of the sentence. The second cell provides information about what the subject does by giving us a VERB. The third then provides further information by giving us an OBJECT; it tells us, for example, what Mary writes.

Each of the sentences above contains three sentence components: subject, verb, object:

SUBJECT	VERB	OBJECT
Mary	writes	books

Phrases

As you can see from the example sentences, sometimes the subject or object is a single word (e.g. *Martin*) and sometimes it is a group of words (e.g. *Our friends at number 29*). In grammar, groups of words that form part of a sentence pattern are called PHRASES. So in the last of the three examples each of these groups of words forms a phrase:

Our **friends** at number 29

are visiting

their **relatives** in Australia.

A phrase is a group of words built up on a single word. In the examples above that single word, or HEADWORD, is printed in bold type. If the headword is a noun, then the phrase is called a NOUN PHRASE. *Our friends at number 29* and *their relatives in Australia* are both noun phrases; *are visiting* is a verb phrase. Another very common type of phrase is the PREPOSITIONAL PHRASE. Prepositional phrases always begin with a preposition. Prepositions are words placed before a noun or noun phrase and they give information about position, time, and other things. Examples are:

in   at   up   before

In the example sentences there are two prepositional phrases:

at number 29

in Australia

As you can see, these both form a part of a larger phrase. In each case the prepositional phrase provides more information about the headword of the phrase. If the subject of the sentence were just *our friends*, people might ask, 'Which friends?': *at number 29* answers that question. The fact that some phrases can have other phrases nesting inside them can be confusing at times, but that is the way in which English works.

Sentences and clauses

So far we have looked at how phrases and words build up into sentences. But there is one further level of grammar you have to understand before you can really grasp how sentences work: clauses.

Clauses normally contain a verb, and most contain one or more other components. They follow a number of patterns, and we have already looked at one:

But, you could well object, just now that was described as a

SUBJECT	VERB	OBJECT
Mary	writes	books

sentence. How can it be a sentence and a clause at the same time? The reason is that we can have different kinds of sentence. Some consist of just one clause, like *Mary writes books*, and others consist of several clauses:

CLAUSE	CLAUSE	CLAUSE
Mary writes books.		
Mary writes books	and loves reading them too.	
Although Mary writes books	she has not been very successful	and is looking for another career.

There are two ways of telling whether a group of words is a clause or not:

- it should contain a full verb:

  Although Mary **writes** books

  she **has** not **been** very successful

  and **is looking** for another career

- it should follow one of a number of standard patterns, like SUBJECT + VERB + OBJECT.

Changing words

So far we have looked at four grammatical levels: sentence, clause, phrase, word. There is just one more we need to be aware of. Some words can change their form according to where they are placed in a sentence and how they are used. For example, nouns change their form according to whether they are singular or plural:

house $\rightarrow$ houses

mouse $\rightarrow$ mice

child $\rightarrow$ children

Some personal pronouns have different forms according to whether they are the subject or the object of the sentence:

He was my boss at Sanders & Webb.

I couldn't stand **him**.

These different forms of a word are referred to by grammarians as MORPHEMES. The study of how words change their forms according to use is MORPHOLOGY.

The five levels

The five grammatical levels can be shown in a diagram:

SENTENCES   The children watched a TV programme
                while their mother made the tea.

CLAUSES   The children watched   their mother
                a TV programme   made the tea

PHRASES   The children   watched   a TV programme

WORDS   The   children

MORPHEMES   child   ren

Types of sentence

We can use sentences for four main purposes in communication:

■ to make a statement:

   That car is travelling very fast.

■ to ask a question:

   Is that car breaking the speed limit?

■ to give an order or make a request:

   Don't drive so fast!

■ to make an exclamation:

   How fast that car is travelling!

Each has a different structure, but since statement sentences are by far the commonest, the explanations in this introduction concentrate on them.

Clause components

Clauses can contain five different components:

- subject
- verb
- object
- complement
- adverbial

Subject + verb

The simplest pattern for a clause is a subject followed by a verb. The subject tells us what the sentence is about and the verb tells us what the subject is doing, or has been doing:

SUBJECT	VERB
Birds	sing.
A very large and ugly chicken	was squawking.

Subject + verb + object

If there is an object, it normally follows the verb. It refers to a different person or thing from the subject. Frequently that person or thing is affected by the action described by the verb:

SUBJECT	VERB	OBJECT
I	shot	the sheriff.

Subject + verb + complement

A small number of verbs are followed not by an object, but by a complement. The commonest of these verbs is *be*. For example:

SUBJECT	VERB	COMPLEMENT
I	am	the sheriff.

In clauses like this the verb acts like an equal sign:

I = the sheriff.

The purpose of the complement is to *complete* the subject — hence its name:

SUBJECT	VERB	COMPLEMENT
This book	is	absolutely fascinating.
Peter Smithson	became	Managing Director.
His wife	seemed	very happy.

Subject + verb + object + complement

It is also possible to have part of a clause that completes the object:

SUBJECT	VERB	OBJECT	COMPLEMENT
The company	made	Peter Smithson	Managing Director.
This	made	his wife	very happy.

In these sentences the imaginary equal sign is between the object and its complement:

The company made Peter Smithson = Managing Director.

Subject + verb + object + object

A number of verbs can have not just one but two objects. In the sentence *Miriam gave her brother a present* both *her brother* and *a present* are objects, but in different ways. The two objects answer different questions:

— What did Miriam give?

— A present.

— Whom did she give it to?

— Her brother.

A present is called the DIRECT OBJECT and *her brother* the indirect object.

SUBJECT	VERB	INDIRECT OBJECT	DIRECT OBJECT
Miriam	gave	her brother	a present.
Sinclair & Groves	have sent	me	several letters about it.

This gives us five common clause patterns:

- subject + verb

  Birds sing.

- subject + verb + object

  I shot the sheriff.

- subject + verb + complement

  I am the sheriff.

- subject + verb + object + complement

  The company made Peter Smithson Managing Director.

- subject + verb + indirect object + direct object

  Miriam gave her brother a present.

In each of these patterns each component, subject, verb, etc. is essential; if you remove any of them, you destroy the grammar of the clause and make the sentence either meaningless or difficult to untangle:

I shot

The company Peter Smithson Managing director

gave her brother a present

Adverbials

There remains one clause component that is much less straightforward: adverbials. These are words or phrases that answer questions such as:

- Where?

  here   down the road

- When?

  later   after a few hours

- How?

  slowly   with great difficulty

- Why?

  for the sake of the children   because of the bad weather

In a small number of clauses the adverbial is an essential component, just like a verb or an object; they are required by the type of verb used:

- subject + verb + **adverbial**

  They have been living **on their savings**.

- subject + verb + object + **adverbial**

  I placed the book **on the table**.

If you remove the adverbial from these clauses you destroy their grammar and leave questions unanswered:

— They have been living ...

— How?

— On their savings.

Optional adverbials

More often an adverbial is not essential to the grammar of the clause it is in. In each of the sentences that follow the adverbial is in bold type.

He found a secret passage **behind the fireplace**.

She is **usually** a very happy child.

Last week Mr and Mrs Holt came to see us.

In each case if you remove the adverbial the clause is still grammatical and still makes sense. As the examples show, adverbials can occur in different positions in the clause. Sometimes they can be moved to a different position:

He found a secret passage   behind the fireplace.

Behind the fireplace   he found a secret passage.

This does not mean that they can be placed *anywhere* in the clause. The following arrangement is impossible:

He behind the fireplace found a secret passage.

Simple and multiple sentences

If a sentence consists of one clause it is described as a simple sentence. Each of the following is a simple sentence:

Mary writes books.

She has not been very successful.

She is looking for another career.

If a sentence contains more than one clause it is described as a multiple sentence. Each of the following sentences is multiple:

She has not been very successful and she is looking for another career.

> Although Mary writes books, she has not been very successful.

Compound sentences

Multiple sentences are made by combining clauses. The simplest way of doing this is to use the grammatical equivalent of a plus sign:

> She has not been very successful + she is looking for another career.

The commonest words to do this job are:

> and   but   or

It is possible to string together as many clauses as you like in this way:

> She has not been very successful **and** she is looking for another career, **but** so far she has not had much luck **and** has decided to try a different tack **or** even give up altogether, **but** ….

until your readers either get lost or give up in disgust!

Complex sentences

There is a limit to the meaning you can express with the conjunction *and*. If someone says *She has not been very successful and she is looking for another career*, we can probably work out that looking for another career is a result of not being very successful, but sometimes joining two clauses by *and* can leave the connection to them very unclear:

> The new CEO was appointed and Martin resigned.

This sentence describes two events but it doesn't show what connection there was between them—always supposing there was any connection at all. We could link the two clauses in ways that *did* show a connection. For example:

Before the new CEO was appointed Martin resigned.

After the new CEO was appointed Martin resigned.

Although the new CEO was appointed Martin resigned.

The new CEO was appointed **so** Martin resigned.

and so on.

In compound sentences the clauses joined together are of equal status; we can cut the sentence up into clauses and each of them will become an independent simple sentence. Complex sentences work in a different way. One of the clauses is the **main** clause and the others are **subordinate** to it. The subordinate clauses form a single component of the main clause: subject, object, complement, or adverbial. In the first of each of the pairs of sentences that follow the subordinate clause is in bold type. In the second sentence it has been replaced by a word or short phrase.

■ SUBJECT

What you did yesterday was inexcusable.

It was inexcusable.

■ OBJECT

I cannot forgive **what you did yesterday**.

I cannot forgive **your action**.

■ COMPLEMENT

That is **what I admire about Billie**.

That is **it**.

■ ADVERBIAL

After the new CEO was appointed Martin resigned.

Afterwards Martin resigned.

Oxford
A–Z
of Grammar
and
Punctuation

abbreviations

The presentation of abbreviations in writing raises two questions:

■ Should I use full stops?

■ Do I use capital or small letters?

Full stops

■ Normally if you use initial (first) letters to represent words there is no need to put a full stop after them:

UK   BBC

■ In North America, however, it is more common to use a full stop (or 'period') after initial letters.

■ If the abbreviation consists of the first and last letters of the word, then you do not use a full stop:

Mr   Ltd

■ If the abbreviation consists of the first part of a word, you put a full stop at the end:

Wed.   Dec.

Capital or small letters

Normally if you use the first letter of a word in an abbreviation a capital letter is used:

HND   BAA   HSBC

One well-known exception to this rule is the abbreviation *plc* for public limited company, although this is also sometimes written PLC.

See also ACRONYM.

abstract noun

Nouns can be divided into two groups: concrete and abstract. Concrete nouns refer to people, places, and things that can be experienced using our five senses. Abstract nouns refer to thoughts, ideas, and imaginings that cannot:

CONCRETE	ABSTRACT
man	manliness
table	tabulation
author	authorship

Too many obscure abstractions can make a piece of writing difficult to read. See, for example, the sentence in bold type in the following extract:

> Such people may be keen to work, but unable to find jobs because none are available in their occupation or in their geographical area, so that retraining or rehousing would be necessary to increase the chances of employment. **It could also be that there is a general deficiency of demand for labour throughout the economy, in which case the involuntarily unemployed workers will face fierce competition for the jobs that do become available.**

A general deficiency of demand for labour throughout the economy is just a pompous and long-winded way of saying that there aren't enough jobs to go round. On the other hand there are also many everyday abstract nouns that are simple and direct:

　happiness　　failure　　truth　　beauty

It would be perverse to try to avoid abstract nouns such as these, so the use of abstract nouns in writing is a question of judgement.

acronym

An ABBREVIATION composed of the first letters of other words so that the abbreviation itself forms a word. For example:

> **CRASSH: C**entre for **R**esearch in the **A**rts, **S**ocial **S**ciences, and **H**umanities

> **Aids: a**cquired **i**mmune **d**eficiency **s**yndrome

Acronyms are treated just like ordinary words in a sentence, and may be composed of all capital letters, or of an initial capital followed by small letters. For example:

> Of 34 mothers who gave birth to children with Aids at his hospital, only four had any symptoms of the disease.

> *Daily Telegraph*

a

An abbreviation consisting of initial letters pronounced separately is called an initialism. For example:

WHO   BBC

active voice

TRANSITIVE VERBS (verbs that take an object) can be used in two ways, or 'voices': active and passive:

ACTIVE: The dog bit him.

PASSIVE: He was bitten by the dog.

Transitive verbs usually describe some kind of action. In the sentence *The dog bit him*, you have a person, thing, or idea that performs the action and one that is affected by it. The first is the subject *The dog* and the second the object *him*. When we put a sentence into the passive voice, the object *him* becomes the subject *He*. The original subject *The dog* becomes the agent and has the preposition *by* placed in front of it. In everyday writing the active voice is much more common than the passive.

active or passive?

Using the passive voice has a number of disadvantages. It tends to sound rather formal and remote:

Volunteers were sought to set up the tables.

It can lead to rather complicated expressions:

The opinions of staff and governors were sought and although there were some reservations it was decided that a questionnaire should be distributed to parents.

Sentence 1 would be better as:

They asked for volunteers to set up the tables.

Sentence 2 would be simpler if it were made active:

We asked staff and governors for their views. Although not everyone agreed completely, we decided to send a questionnaire to parents.

▶

a

On the other hand, the passive can make sentences shorter and clearer. For example, this:

> She was run over by a car travelling at excessive speed and overtaking on the wrong side.

is better than:

> A car travelling at excessive speed and overtaking on the wrong side ran her over.

The first sentence has a short subject *She* and is easy to follow. The subject of the second sentence is too long and we lose the sense before we get to the verb.

It + passive

Some writers like to begin a sentence with *It*, followed by the passive. For example, the following sentence concerns the options available to a woman who has been attacked:

> It is considered that in the last resort it is to civil remedies that she should have recourse.

This is 'lawyer talk'. It is better to be direct and use the active voice:

> We believe that in the last resort she will have to sue her attacker.

In some situations, however, the construction can be useful:

> It is believed that similar reserves exist along the coast.

The writer may well not have a clear idea of exactly whose opinion is being quoted, although it is evident that the belief is widespread or well established.

---

addresses

Styles for the presentation of addresses in letters and on envelopes have changed over the years. Contemporary practice is to set addresses with the left hand end of lines square ('left justified') and without any punctuation:

▶

Oxford University Press
Great Clarendon Street
Oxford
OX2 6DP

The postcode is placed separately, on a line of its own, except in the case of London addresses, where it is normally placed on the same line as *London*:

London WC1 6GE

Forms of address

The commonest titles used in addresses are:

Miss   Mr   Mrs   Ms

Mr and *Mrs* are straightforward to use. *Mr* is used for all men who have no other title, while *Mrs* is used for married women. Women who are not married can be addressed in letters as *Miss*, but some women prefer *Ms*. A number of married women also prefer to be addressed as *Ms*. If you are in a situation where you do not know the preferences of the person you are writing to, then it is safest to use *Mrs* for married women and *Ms* for unmarried women.

Increasingly, however, these forms of address are omitted; instead many people prefer to use a first name followed by a surname. The title *Miss* particularly is much less used than it was in the past.

The commonest professional title is *Dr* for doctors (both medical doctors and people who have a higher university degree). Members of the clergy are addressed as *The Reverend*, abbreviated to *Revd* (or *Rev.*).
See also ABBREVIATIONS.

adjective

Adjectives are words that refer to the qualities of people, things, or ideas, or which group them into classes.

a

- Most adjectives can be used with a noun and usually come immediately before it in the sentence:

    a **blue** flower

    a **slow** train

- When adjectives are used in this way they are said to MODIFY the noun; this use is called ATTRIBUTIVE.

- Most adjectives can be used after verbs like *be*, *seem*, *appear* in sentences like this:

    The test was **positive**.

- In such sentences the adjective forms the COMPLEMENT of the sentence and completes the meaning of the sentence SUBJECT. This use is called PREDICATIVE.

- Many adjectives can be GRADED by adding a modifier before or after them:

    a   very   slow   grower
          | |
       MODIFIER ADJECTIVE

- Many adjectives have a comparative and a superlative form:

ABSOLUTE	COMPARATIVE	SUPERLATIVE
sad	sadder	saddest
unusual	more unusual	most unusual

But ...

- Some adjectives can only be used predicatively; they cannot be used attributively. You can say:

    She was alone.

- but you cannot say:

    I saw an alone woman.

- Some adjectives can only be used attributively; they cannot be used predicatively. You can say:

    It was a mere skirmish.

- but you cannot say:

    The skirmish was mere.

Qualitative and classifying

Some adjectives describe the qualities of a person, thing, or idea; they tell us about its qualities — whether it was large or small, red or green. For example:

a **stupendous** achievement

an **exciting** proposal

These are referred to as qualitative adjectives.

Other adjectives help to divide persons, things, or ideas into classes; they tell us which of a number of groups they fall into — nuclear or non-nuclear? annual, biennial, or triennial?

the **French** language

an **annual** event

Such classifying adjectives cannot usually be graded and they do not normally have comparative or superlative forms. So it would be odd to say, for example:

It was a very annual event.

Using commas

When two or more adjectives are used in a list the question arises: should they be separated by commas? There are no clear-cut rules about this but the following guidelines may help.

No comma is needed to separate adjectives of different types, e.g. a qualitative and a classifying adjective:

a big black dog

Use a comma between two or more qualitative adjectives:

long, slender legs

If the adjectives are all classifying adjectives, use commas if the adjectives all refer to the same class:

English, French, and Spanish editions

a tall, conical lid

Otherwise do not use commas:

Italian Renaissance architecture.

adjective phrase

An adjective phrase is a group of words built up round an adjective. There are two main ways in which this is done.

■ An ADVERB is placed in front of the adjective:

'He's a	very	remarkable	man,' said Alison.
	ADVERB	ADJECTIVE	
	ADJECTIVE PHRASE		

The adverb MODIFIES the adjective by changing its meaning. *Very* is the commonest adverb used in this way. Others are:

rather   quite   fairly

You can have more than one adverb in front of the adjective. For example:

I'm **really rather** busy at the moment.

■ Sometimes words are placed after the adjective to modify it in a similar way:

ADJECTIVE	MODIFIER(S)
slow	enough
intrigued	by the project

adjunct

Adjuncts are ADVERBIALS that add more information to a sentence. They can provide additional information about:

■ where things happen

At low tide you can cross the bays **on the beach**.

■ when things happen

I cannot sleep **at night**.

■ how things happen

I found out how to do this **by accident**.

■ why things happen

No one is turned away **because of a lack of means**.

■ the purpose of an action

I still send her a Christmas card each year **for old times' sake**.

- condition (If this happens, then that happens.)

    Leslie had left no letter for me to read **in the event of his death**.
- concession (Even if this happens, still that happens.)

    Despite all its efforts, America still has its racists.
- degree (Answering the question 'How much?')

    I wouldn't worry **at all**.

adverb

Adverbs constitute a WORD CLASS or PART OF SPEECH.

Use as adverbials

They are often used as sentence ADVERBIALS, or ADJUNCTS, providing information about, for example, place, time, and manner:

- PLACE

    here   away   somewhere
- TIME

    soon   already   still
- MANNER

    easily   deftly   slowly

Use with adjectives and other adverbs

Adverbs can also be used to MODIFY adjectives and thus form ADJECTIVE PHRASES:

ADVERB	ADJECTIVE
very	easy
rather	attractive

They can work in a similar way with other adverbs to make ADVERB PHRASES:

ADVERB	ADVERB
quite	soon
extremely	slowly

Formation

Many adverbs are formed from adjectives by adding –*ly*:

slow + ly → slowly

Not all adverbs end in –*ly*, and some of the commonest adverbs are not formed in this way. For example:

afterwards   rather   very

See also ADVERB FORMATION.

adverb formation

Many ADJECTIVES can be transformed into ADVERBS by the addition of the SUFFIX -*ly*.

Rules

■ The base rule is that you add –*ly* to the adjective:

sad → sadly

■ If the adjective ends in –*ll*, just add –*y*:

full → fully

■ Most adjectives of one syllable that end in –*y* are regular, with the exception of *gay* → *gaily*

■ For two-syllable adjectives that end in –*y*, replace the final -*y* with the letters -*ily*:

happy → happily

■ Adjectives that end with a consonant followed by –*le*, replace the final -*e* with -*y*:

terrible → terribly

■ Adjectives that end in –*ly* cannot be transformed by adding –*ly*. Instead, use a short phrase:

friendly → in a friendly way

adverb phrase

A group of words built up round an adverb by adding words before and/or after it. For example:

	ADVERB	
very	smoothly	
as	economically	as possible

adverbial

A single word or a group of words that forms part of a CLAUSE. There are three types of adverbial:

■ ADJUNCTS. These provide additional information. For example:

It is safe to climb up or down either path **at walking pace**.

■ CONJUNCTS. These provide a link between sentences:

It wasn't as if I even wanted to sit down and write in the first place. I have no training as a writer. I don't believe that telling a story is as easy as it looks. **Moreover**, this story is a painful one for me to tell.

■ DISJUNCTS. You use these to make your own comments on the information you are communicating:

Unfortunately it is unlikely that your boss will change his ways.

An adverbial may be a single word, in which case it is usually an ADVERB — for example *unfortunately*. An adverbial can also be a group of words like *at walking pace*.

adverbial clause

In COMPLEX SENTENCES adverbial clauses provide information about:

■ CONCESSION

Clare has seen it, **although she probably hasn't had time to read it fully**.

■ CONDITION

If you see a stranger acting suspiciously outside your home or your neighbour's call the police.

■ MANNER

I called him as usual, and he answered with his usual whinny but made no effort to come to me **as he normally did**.

a

■ PLACE

Where the river straightened, he took his chance to check the barometer.

■ PURPOSE

They joined a major label **so that they could sell records throughout the world.**

■ REASON

Yet, **perhaps because it was not televised,** it produced mighty little stir.

■ RESULT

This was written **so** quickly **that several errors occurred.**

■ TIME

When dawn broke, the rain ceased and the various parties were able to take stock of their positions.

adverbial position

Beginning or end

An ADVERBIAL can come at the beginning or end of a CLAUSE or SENTENCE. For example:

After several hours of random identity checks the troops dispersed.

The troops dispersed **after several hours of random identity checks.**

This does not mean that all adverbials can take both positions. For example, while you can say

The trees rushed past **at great speed.**

you cannot say

At great speed the trees rushed past.

This is because the adverbial *at great speed* refers particularly to the action described by the verb *rushed*, and this link is destroyed if you separate it from the verb.

▶

a

Middle

Adverbials can also be placed in the middle of the sentence. This is particularly true of single word adverbials or ADVERBS. The key to placing the adverbial correctly is the VERB. If the verb consists of a single word, then the adverbial is usually placed immediately before it:

>   They **finally** reached the deck.

If there is an AUXILIARY VERB and a MAIN VERB the adverb is placed between them:

>   They   have   **finally**   reached   the deck.
>
>   AUXILIARY VERB   ADVERB   MAIN VERB

In such sentences, adverbials cannot be placed between the main verb and its OBJECT:

>   They have reached finally the deck.

Adverbials can also cause difficulties when they are used with an INFINITIVE, sometimes leading to a SPLIT INFINITIVE.

after

This word commonly refers to time, helping us to explain the order in which events happen:

>   She went back to work very quickly **after** her operation.

It can also sometimes refer to space, usually helping place people or things in order:

>   'Where are you going?' said Lee, coming **after** him.

After can be:

■ a PREPOSITION:

>   **After** his election Dr Kumar spoke of the racial attacks he endured during the campaign.

■ a SUBORDINATING CONJUNCTION:

>   **After** he was elected in November, he revealed that he had been the subject of racial attacks during his campaign.

a

■ an ADVERB:

> Then he spun around and strode out of the door, his men
> following **after** without a word.

It is also used to MODIFY a NOUN in phrases such as *the morning
after*.

after/afterwards

In formal writing, *after* should not be used as an adverb of time.
Instead use *afterwards*:

> It was not so easy to brush him off **afterwards**.

not

> It was not so easy to brush him off **after**.

The exception to this is when it follows a word or phrase giving a
measure of time. For example:

> But what about the year **after**?

agreement

The SUBJECT and the VERB of a clause have to **agree** in NUMBER
and PERSON.

PERSON	NUMBER	PRONOUN(S)	TO BE	TO WRITE
1st	singular	I	am	write
1st	plural	we	are	write
2nd	singular	you	are	write
2nd	plural	you	are	write
3rd	singular	he, she, it	is	writes
3rd	plural	they	are	write

Writers sometimes fail to make the verb of a sentence agree
with the subject. This usually happens when the subject of the
sentence is a lengthy NOUN PHRASE. For example:

▶

> The advent of digitization and electronic media **make**
> speedy cooperation between us even more necessary.
>
> This should be:
>
> The advent of digitization and electronic media **makes**
> speedy cooperation between us even more necessary.
>
> The rule is that the verb should agree with the main word in
> the subject, the HEADWORD of the phrase. If in doubt, you
> should try to boil the subject down to a single noun or
> pronoun. In this case the subject boils down to *advent*, which
> is singular.

also

This is an adverb, used to link items in a sentence or to make links
between sentences. For example:

> The oxygen they produce benefits the fish, and they **also**
> provide a source of food and shelter.

It is frequently used with *and* or *but*, but it is not a conjunction. In
formal writing *also* should not be used instead of *and*:

> The closet is larger than a pit and therefore lasts longer **also** it is
> easy to empty.

Here the speaker needs to add *and* (→ *and also*), or replace *also*
with *and*.

and

A COORDINATING CONJUNCTION which is used to join two items.
These can be:

■ two words:

> bread **and** butter
>
> to **and** fro

■ two PHRASES:

> eight European countries **and** a number of international
> agencies

■ TWO CLAUSES:

> Then he rolled off the seat into the footwell **and** immediately started snoring again.

antonym

A word meaning the opposite of another word. For example, the following are pairs of antonyms:

wet	dry
buy	sell
child	adult

See also SYNONYM.

any

A word that can be used in these ways:

■ DETERMINER

> I sat in my cell, expecting to be called out for execution at **any** moment.

■ PRONOUN

> I don't think there'll be **any** to spare for a day or two.

■ ADVERB. It can be used before the COMPARATIVE form of an ADJECTIVE or ADVERB. For example:

> Why won't the car go **any** faster?

apostrophe

The apostrophe is the punctuation mark which causes more people more problems than any other. It is used for two purposes:

To show that one or more letters have been missed out

When we are speaking we frequently elide certain sounds, running parts of a word together. For example, *did not* becomes *didn't*. When these words are written down, an apostrophe is used to show that letters have been missed out:

will not	→	won't
shall not	→	shan't
might have	→	might've
she is	→	she's
they are	→	they're

As the examples show, the way in which some of these shortened forms are written down is rather selective. It works well when *is* and *are* are shortened, but in the case of *won't* and *shan't*, the apostrophe does not show where all the letters have been omitted; otherwise we would write *sha'n't*, and no rule can cover the change from *will not* to *won't*.

To show possession

We also use the apostrophe to show that something belongs to someone. For example:

Lord Rochester's monkey

the girl's handbag

the Browns' Silver Wedding anniversary

several churches' position on gay priests

As these examples show, the rule is that if the name or noun is in the singular, we add an apostrophe followed by the letter 's'. If the name or noun is a plural ending in 's' then we simply add an apostrophe. (Plurals that do not end in 's' follow the rule for singular nouns: *a children's playground*.)

Exception

There is one exception to the rule. When *its* means 'of it' there is no apostrophe. This commonly causes problems. The rule is:

■ *it's* = it is

■ *its* = of it

apposition

It is possible to place one NOUN or NOUN PHRASE next to another one in a sentence, so that it explains or amplifies it. For example:

The writer Michael Viney left Dublin 13 years ago to live a life of peace and self-sufficiency in a remote house.

a

Here the short phrases *the writer* and *Michael Viney* work in parallel. They are said to be in **apposition** to each other.

In the example above, the sentence would work grammatically with only one of the phrases:

> The writer left Dublin 13 years ago to live a life of peace and self-sufficiency in a remote house.

> Michael Viney left Dublin 13 years ago to live a life of peace and self-sufficiency in a remote house.

But neither of these alternative versions is completely satisfactory. The first leads us to ask, 'Which writer?', while the second prompts: 'Who is Michael Viney?'

See also PARENTHESIS.

article

A term used in traditional grammar. It consists of these words:

a, an	indefinite article
the	definite article

Articles form part of a larger group of words known as DETERMINERS.

as

A word that can be used in three main ways:

Subordinating conjunction

It can introduce a number of different types of ADVERBIAL CLAUSE:

■ Time

> **As** the train drew into Victoria station, Gloria softened.

■ Reason

> **As** they are fast-drying ... the application technique is slightly different.

■ Manner

> The talk that night was about experiments carried out to explain why people behaved **as** they did.

■ Comment

That, **as** I understand it, is the law.

The commonest of these four uses are the first two; in them *as* can mean 'while' or 'because'. Occasionally this can cause confusion if a sentence is carelessly constructed. For example:

I left the farm as it was getting late.

Does this mean *when it was getting late*, or *because it was getting late*?

Preposition

Should I get a job **as** a barmaid?

Adverb

It can also be used as an adverb in comparisons:

He's **as** happy **as** a sandboy.

auxiliary verb

A group of verbs that combine with the MAIN VERB to form the VERB PHRASE:

Primary	be	is	am	are	was	were	been
	have	has	had				
Modal	shall	will	should	would			
	can	could					
	may	might					
	must						
	ought (to)						

See also MODAL AUXILIARY VERBS, PRIMARY AUXILIARY VERBS.

base

The word or part of a word to which PREFIXES and SUFFIXES are attached to form new words. In the words that follow, the base is printed in bold type.

counter**act** under**achieve**ment un**necessari**ly un**happi**ness

before

A word with two main uses:

■ SUBORDINATING CONJUNCTION. It introduces CLAUSES OF TIME. For example:

> He wanted to see her **before** it was too late.

■ PREPOSITION

> I hardly expected you **before** midnight.

brackets

A pair of punctuation marks used to indicate that the words enclosed are not essential to the meaning of the sentence, but provide additional information:

> He coined the term *hypnotism* **(from the Greek *hypnos*, meaning 'sleep')** and practised it frequently.

The words enclosed in brackets are described as being in PARENTHESIS.

Brackets can be used to enclose additional information that doesn't fit into the grammatical structure of the sentence. For example:

> It's like any group of people **(virtual or in real life)**; you're going to have individuals who feel a certain way about an issue...

Brackets are also used by some writers to make asides, comments to the reader which do not form part of the main argument or story being expressed. For example:

> This is also known as junk email ... or spam. Obviously, it's impossible to distribute processed lunchmeat electronically at this time **(and hopefully it'll never happen)**.

In informal writing this is intended to make readers feel that the writer is talking directly to them, and it can be effective. But if it is used too much it quickly becomes irritating.

See also PARENTHESIS.

b

building texts

When we write any text that consists of more than one sentence we use a number of techniques to ensure that it holds together. This is done in two main ways:

■ Structure
■ Cohesion

Structure

Different kinds of writing require different structures. A personal letter is organized very differently from a newspaper report. But all have a structure and most use PARAGRAPHS. The way in which one paragraph leads into the next is an essential part of the way in which text is built.

Cohesion

We also use vocabulary and grammar to help 'glue' our sentences together and make life easier for the reader. There are three main devices we use:

1. REFERENCE. We use certain types of word to refer back to things that have already been explained. The commonest of these are PRONOUNS. For example:

> When we write any text that consists of more than one sentence we use a number of techniques to ensure that **it** holds together. **This** is done in two main ways ...

The words *it* and *this* make the sentence shorter. Otherwise we would have to write:

> When we write any text that consists of more than one sentence we use a number of techniques to ensure that **the text** holds together. **Making sure that the text holds together** is done in two main ways ...

Using pronouns in this way not only makes the writing shorter, it also links sentences closely together.

▶

b

2. ELLIPSIS. It is also possible to miss out single words and phrases or replace them with much shorter forms. For example:

As it turned out, I knew the Bible better than he **did**.

This is a shorter version of the much more long-winded:

As it turned out, I knew the Bible better than he **knew the Bible**.

Again, not only is it shorter, but also by referring back to the reader's previous knowledge, it gives the sentence cohesion.

3. SENTENCE ADVERBIALS. These are words or short phrases that show how parts of a text link together. They do this in a number of different ways. For example:

■ Making lists

First you have to think of it and **secondly** you have to say it.

■ Giving examples

In addition, students choose from other units in which the emphasis is on a particular aspect or approach to history, **for example** the history of the Origins of Modern Science.

■ Explaining cause or result

Unemployment rises and so increases the army of industrial reserves: **as a result** wages are driven down even further.

but

A COORDINATING CONJUNCTION used to link together:

■ two ADJECTIVES:

tired but happy

■ two PHRASES:

nice to look at but difficult to describe

■ two CLAUSES:

> You begin by admiring but it soon grows boring.

can

A MODAL AUXILIARY VERB. It has two meanings:

■ That someone or something has the ability to do something:

> Those who **can** swim, swim.

■ That something is possible:

> I suppose anything **can** happen now.

can/may

Traditionally *can* is used to show:

■ ability

> An English person who **can** speak even one other language fluently is rare.

■ possibility

> Relapse can occur at any time.

May is normally used to show:

■ permission

> Candidates **may** enter for both examinations, if desired.

■ possibility

> It **may** cause pain, but often there are no symptoms.

Today *can* is increasingly used to show permission:

> Mum, **can** I leave it?

Using *can* in this way is accepted as standard English, although many people still use *may* in more formal situations.

capital letters

Capital letters are used for the following purposes:

■ For the first letter of a sentence:

> Expenditure rises to meet income.

- For the first letters of the names of people, places, and special days:

    Nelson Mandela   Hong Kong   New Year's Day

- For the first letters of the main words of the titles of books, plays, newspapers, and magazines:

    Much Ado About Nothing   New York Herald Tribune

- For the first letters of the main words of the titles of people and institutions:

    the Prime Minister   the Houses of Parliament

- In ABBREVIATIONS:

    USA   HSBC

case

NOUNS and PRONOUNS can be used as the SUBJECT or the OBJECT of a sentence:

SUBJECT	VERB	OBJECT
The dog	bit	her.
She	sold	her dog.

As can be seen from this example, the pronoun *she* is used as the subject, but if it is used as the object it becomes *her*. These different forms are called cases. There are three cases in English, subjective, objective, and possessive:

SUBJECTIVE	OBJECTIVE	POSSESSIVE
I	me	mine
we	us	ours
she	her	hers
he	him	his
it	it	its
you	you	yours
they	them	theirs
who	whom	whose

The subjective form is used for the subject of a clause or sentence and also, in formal language, for the SUBJECT COMPLEMENT (for example, *It is I*). The objective form is used for the object and also after prepositions (for example, *The person to whom I gave a present*...). The possessive form is used in sentences such as:

England is **mine**. It owes me a living.

You have my soul now, all my thoughts are **yours**.

In some languages nouns have subjective and objective cases, but English nouns do not. They do, however, have a possessive case. We add an APOSTROPHE followed by the letter 's' to show this in singular nouns and add a simple apostrophe to plurals ending in 's':

a person's name

my parents' Silver Wedding

---

clauses

SENTENCES can consist of one or more clauses. Their part in grammatical structure is shown in this diagram:

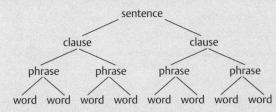

Clauses are made up of two or more clause components:

- SUBJECT
- VERB
- OBJECT
- COMPLEMENT
- ADVERBIAL

▶

All clauses used to make a statement normally contain a subject and a verb, in that order. They may also contain one or more additional components. All English clauses are based on one of seven basic patterns:

	subject	verb		
1	**subject**	**verb**		
	The sun	rose.		
2	**subject**	**verb**	**complement**	
	The light	was	low.	
3	**subject**	**verb**	**adverbial**	
	It	came	from the east.	
4	**subject**	**verb**	**object**	
	He	saw	the dawn.	
5	**subject**	**verb**	**object**	**object**
	He	gave	the dog	a bone.
6	**subject**	**verb**	**object**	**adverbial**
	It	took	it	away.
7	**subject**	**verb**	**object**	**complement**
	This	made	him	happy.

Clauses can be FINITE or NON-FINITE. All the examples above are finite clauses.

See also NON-FINITE CLAUSE.

coherence and cohesion

If you write more than one or two sentences on a subject, you have to ensure that your text holds together and makes sense to your readers. You do this by making sure that it has two important qualities:

■ coherence

■ cohesion

Coherence

Coherence means that the thought behind the text is consistent and moves logically from one point to the next. A coherent text uses suitable vocabulary and uses it consistently.

Cohesion

The use of grammatical devices to make sure that a text sticks together. The commonest of these are:

- REFERENCE
- ELLIPSIS
- SENTENCE ADVERBIALS

See also BUILDING A TEXT.

collective noun

A singular noun that refers to several individuals. For example:

the police   the choir   Parliament

The main question raised by collective nouns is AGREEMENT: do you use a singular or a plural verb? Is it *the jury is …* or *the jury are …?* The answer is: it depends on the context. If the speaker is thinking of the jury as a united body, then the singular is used:

The selection jury **is** chaired by London's Roy Miles.

If the jury is being thought of as a group of separate individuals, then the plural is used:

The jury **are** about to hear it from the witness.

It is important to be consistent. So the example above should not be continued as follows:

The selection jury **is** chaired by London's Roy Miles. **They include** several famous people.

It should be:

The selection jury **is** chaired by London's Roy Miles. **It includes** several famous people.

colon

A punctuation mark with three main uses:

- to introduce a list:

    There are two other varieties of cedarwood oil: Texas (*Juniperus ashei*) and Virginian (*Juniperus virginiana*).

- to introduce a piece of direct speech, or a quotation:

    At once he said: 'I do not mean your immediate brief journey.'

- to separate two parts of a sentence where the first leads on to the second:

> And that is the end of the poor man's hopes: there is no return to eligibility.

See also COMMAS, COLONS, AND SEMICOLONS.

comma

This punctuation mark has the following uses:

- to separate the items in a list:

> ... tens of thousands of them: Christians, Hindus, Muslims, Sikhs.

- to place a section of a sentence in PARENTHESIS (as brackets do):

> Bill the dog, happy as ever to be out and about, was sniffing everything in sight.

- to mark the divisions between the CLAUSES in a COMPLEX SENTENCE:

> These weedkillers may, if used on new lawns, damage young seedling grasses before they are well established.

- to separate sections of a sentence to make it easier to read:

> To make a hot compress, pour hot water into a bowl and then add the essential oil.

- to introduce and/or end a piece of direct speech:

> 'No, sir,' said Stephen, 'and that is what is so curious.'

You do not need to use a comma between nouns that are in APPOSITION:

> my wife Dorothy

> Alison and her friend Beth were attracted to the same man at a party.

Commas should be used to surround a noun that is in PARENTHESIS:

> Pete, his son, cleaned the garden aviary.

Use a comma when writing a number that is made up of four or more figures:

> 23,500   1,500 miles

but not in dates:

> 1 May 2004   the 1970s

commas, colons, and semicolons

These three punctuation marks are all used to mark off different sections within a sentence. It is sometimes difficult to decide which to use. The decision is sometimes a matter of personal style, but the guidelines that follow will help in a large number of cases. The separate entries for the three punctuation marks contain additional information.

■ When introducing a piece of direct speech a comma is used much more frequently than a colon. A colon can be used for special effect:

> Intrigue is our mother's milk. We say: 'He is an excellent fellow, but ...'

A colon is also used to introduce an extended quotation.

■ Commas are normally used between the items in a list, unless each item is quite extensive. If so, a semicolon is used:

> Weeds may reach the lawn in various ways: as seeds blown by the wind; carried by birds; brought in on muddy footwear, machinery, or tools; or concealed in unsterilized soil or badly made compost used for top dressing.

■ A semicolon marks a much stronger division within a sentence than a comma. It can be used to separate two sections which might otherwise form separate sentences. The sections separated in this way are normally FINITE CLAUSES.

> The essential oil found in jasmine flowers is too delicate to be produced by distillation; the heat tends to destroy the odour.

In the sentence above, the semicolon could be replaced by a full stop, but this would separate two ideas that are closely related. As it stands the sentence has a clear balance, with separate but linked ideas pivoting on the semicolon. It is wrong to use a comma to link sections of a sentence in this way.

■ If the first part of a sentence introduces an idea which appears in the second part, then a colon is better than a semicolon:

▶

> Many consumers are against it: about three out of ten say
> it's never a good thing, and most others see it as an
> occasional necessity rather than as having positive
> advantages.

common noun

NOUNS can be divided into two groups, common nouns and
PROPER NOUNS. Proper nouns are those that refer to people,
places, and things that are unique, for example *Manchester* and
William Shakespeare. All nouns that are not proper nouns are
grouped together as common nouns.

comparative

The form of an adjective that is used when comparing things. For
example:

He is **taller** than me.

The comparative is formed in different ways according to the
length of the base adjective:

■ If it has one syllable, then the letters *-er* are added.

■ If the word has three syllables or more, then the word 'more' is
added before the adjective: *more attractive*.

■ Words of two syllables vary: some add *-er* and some use 'more'.
Some can do either, for example *clever*.

The use of 'more' and adding *-er* are alternatives. It is wrong to use
both together (e.g. *more better*).

Spelling: adding -er

■ If the word ends in a consonant, add *–er* (*quick* becomes *quicker*).

■ With words of one syllable with a short vowel sound and ending
with a single consonant, double the consonant and add *–er* (*sad*
becomes *sadder*).

■ With words of one syllable ending in *–l*, you normally do **not**
double the *l*, but *cruel* becomes *crueller*.

■ If it ends in 'e', add *–r* (*late* becomes *later*).

■ If it ends in 'y', change the 'y' to an 'i' and add *–er* (*happy* becomes *happier*).

complement

A clause component that completes an earlier part. Clauses can have a SUBJECT COMPLEMENT:

It	is	a shy forest animal.
SUBJECT	VERB	**SUBJECT COMPLEMENT**

or an OBJECT COMPLEMENT:

It	made	him	angry and irritable.
SUBJECT	VERB	OBJECT	**OBJECT COMPLEMENT**

complex sentence

A sentence with a MAIN CLAUSE and at least one SUBORDINATE CLAUSE introduced by a SUBORDINATING CONJUNCTION. Examples of complex sentences are:

She told him	that	she did not play again for over a week.
MAIN CLAUSE	SUBORDINATING CONJUNCTION	SUBORDINATE CLAUSE

If	it rains	everything in the shed will get wet.
SUBORDINATING CONJUNCTION	SUBORDINATE CLAUSE	MAIN CLAUSE

When	the children came back from school	they found	that	still nothing had changed.
SUBORDINATING CONJUNCTION	SUBORDINATE CLAUSE	MAIN CLAUSE	SUBORDINATING CONJUNCTION	SUBORDINATE CLAUSE

compound sentence

A sentence with two or more main clauses joined by a
COORDINATING CONJUNCTION. Examples of compound sentences
are:

Then he came in	and	she sat down quickly.	
MAIN CLAUSE	COORDINATING CONJUNCTION	MAIN CLAUSE	
Either	you agree with it	or	you don't agree with it.
COORDINATING CONJUNCTION	MAIN CLAUSE	COORDINATING CONJUNCTION	MAIN CLAUSE

compound word

A word composed of two other words. Examples include:

crime reporter   fortune-teller   scarecrow

As the examples show, the two words that form the compound
are sometimes written separately, sometimes linked by a hyphen,
and sometimes joined together. For many compounds there is a
standard way, but other compounds are written in more than one
way. For example:

paper knife   paper-knife   paperknife

In modern English there is a tendency to avoid the hyphenated
version if possible and use either a single word or two words. In the
United States people often prefer a single word (for example *airfare*),
while in Britain two words are preferred (for example *air fare*).

See also HYPHEN.

concession

To concede something is to admit its truth, usually after you have
originally denied it or refused to admit that it may be true. An
ADVERBIAL or ADVERBIAL CLAUSE of concession is one that says in
effect, 'Yes, even though A was true, B happened.'

Adverbial clauses of concession

There are three main types:

■ Beginning with the CONJUNCTION *although*:

Although she always wanted to be a writer, SUBORDINATE CLAUSE	the theatre has claimed a lot of her energy. MAIN CLAUSE

The writer finds the information contained in the main clause (that she has worked a lot in the theatre) surprising in the light of the subordinate clause (that she wanted to be a writer).

■ In another type of concession clause the information contained in the subordinate clause may well be true, but it doesn't affect the truth of the information in the main clause:

Even if she took it into her head to come back early, SUBORDINATE CLAUSE	she wouldn't be back till half four at the earliest. MAIN CLAUSE

■ In a third type the main clause contains information that is true, *despite* the truth of the information in the subordinate clause:

Tom supplements their pension by working part-time, MAIN CLAUSE	even though he is nearly 70. SUBORDINATE CLAUSE

The main conjunctions used to introduce adverbial clauses of concession are:

    although   despite   even if   even though   except that

    not that   though   whereas   while   whilst

It is also possible to have NON-FINITE CLAUSES of concession. For example:

    In spite of being so fair, his skin had taken on quite a deep tan in the few days they had been there.

There are also verbless clauses of concession:

    Although a competent fighter, Stretch was not considered to be one of the game's bigger punchers.

Adverbials of concession

Sentences may also contain phrases which express similar ideas to clauses of concession.

> It had been a happy marriage, **in spite of the difference in their ages**.

> This works **even with the quickest and most agile spiders**.

> **Even after her wedding**, the Princess of Wales continued to shop at Laura Ashley, **albeit with a bodyguard**, and whatever items she bought received wide coverage.

concord

Another word for AGREEMENT.

concrete noun

A NOUN which refers to something which can be seen, touched, heard, tasted, and/or smelled. Concrete nouns are contrasted with ABSTRACT nouns.

condition

When writing or speaking we often wish to show that one event depends on another in some way:

> If the weather was fine, Maud liked to walk in Hyde Park.

One statement, *Maud liked to walk in Hyde Park*, is **conditional** upon the other *the weather was fine*.

Conditional clauses are usually introduced by either *if* or *unless*. They can express a number of different meanings.

Common events

They can state general truths, such as:

> **If water penetrates window sills, doors, or their frames,** the result is wet rot.

In sentences like this the verb is in the present tense. It is also possible to use the past tense to describe general truths about the past:

> **If the weather was fine**, Maud liked to walk in Hyde Park.

Possible events

Conditional clauses can describe situations which have not yet happened, but are possible:

> **If it comes to court**, you two can testify.

Here both verbs are in the present tense. Similar sentences can be constructed using *unless*:

> Policemen don't find bodies **unless they are sent to look for them** or **unless someone else has found them first**.

Here *unless* has the meaning of *if ... not ...*:

> Policemen don't find bodies **if they aren't sent to look for them** or **if someone else hasn't found them first**.

Future events

Very often conditional clauses speculate about events in the future. Such clauses can be open or closed. In an open conditional the speaker expresses no opinion about whether the future event is likely to happen or not:

> **If they succeed in that**, Germany's economy and its workers will be better off.

(The writer has no opinion of whether they will succeed or not.) In a closed condition the writer makes it clear that the future event is more or less unlikely:

> **If they were successful at this stage**, they would then have to find the fee.

(But they are not likely to be successful.)

Past events

Conditional clauses can also be used to speculate about how things might have turned out in the past:

> **If they had been her own children**, she would have used them differently.

But they weren't her own children, so she treated them as she did. The condition cannot be fulfilled because it is impossible.

Clauses that are not introduced by a conjunction

It is possible to construct conditional clauses that do not begin with *if* or *unless*. The commonest way of doing this is to begin the clause with one of these words:

were   should   had

For example:

Were I to own a new BMW car, another ten microcomputers would be at my command, so their advertisements claim.

Should you succeed in becoming a planner, you would be helping to create these parameters.

Had I been in a vehicle, I could have gone back, but on foot it was not worth risking the wasted energy.

conjunct

A type of adverbial used to show the connection between a sentence and an earlier sentence. Common conjuncts include:

above all	again	also	anyhow/anyway
besides	consequently	finally	first for
example	furthermore	however	in addition
in conclusion	in contrast	last(ly)	likewise
moreover	nevertheless	next	otherwise
rather	similarly	so	still then
therefore	though	thus	yet

See also BUILDING A TEXT.

conjunction

A class of words that are used to join together WORDS, PHRASES, or CLAUSES. They fall into two groups.

Coordinating conjunctions

These link items that have equal status grammatically:

uncomfortable **but** safe

ice cream **or** frozen yoghurt

Helena arrived **and** they called room service.

Subordinating conjunctions

If the two items do not have equal status, then a subordinating conjunction is used. Most commonly this happens in COMPLEX SENTENCES when a main clause is joined to a SUBORDINATE CLAUSE:

Businesses fail	because	they can't pay their bills.
MAIN CLAUSE	SUBORDINATING CONJUNCTION	SUBORDINATE CLAUSE

connective

A sentence adverbial, an ADJUNCT, or a CONJUNCT.

consonant

Writing

There are 21 consonant letters:

b c d f g h j k l m n p q r s t v w x y z

Speech

In speech a consonant is a sound that is made by blocking the flow of air while speaking. For example, the first sound in the word *mark* is made by closing the lips briefly, while the last sound is made by pressing the blade of the tongue up against the hard palate. There are 22 consonants in spoken English. They are the first sounds in each of the following words:

bat	char	cut	dip	fat	gut	hot
jar	late	meet	neat	pat	rate	ship
sip	that	thing	tip	vat	zip	

plus the sounds in the following words marked by letters in bold type:

measure   si**ng**

Two other sounds are sometimes called consonants and sometimes semivowels. They are the first sounds in these words:

win   young

content word

Words can be divided into content words like *tree* and STRUCTURE words such as *because*. Content words are:

- NOUNS
- VERBS
- ADJECTIVES
- ADVERBS

conversion

The process by which a word from one WORD CLASS is used as if it belonged to another class. For example, *glue* started life as a NOUN, but is now frequently used as a VERB. Many conversions are so common that we no longer notice them, but conversion is also a feature of creative uses of language:

'I really have some severe doubts regarding this partnership,' said he, **upping** and **awaying**.

It is often said that 'there is no noun in English that can't be verbed'. (Tom McArthur)

coordinating conjunction

A CONJUNCTION that joins two items of the same grammatical status. The commonest coordinating conjunctions are:

and   but   or

They can be used to link WORDS:

biscuits **or** chocolate

PHRASES:

sports shops **and** large department stores

or CLAUSES:

I am working part-time, **but** my maternity leave begins next month.

could

A MODAL AUXILIARY VERB, the past form of *can*. It can refer to ability in sentences that are about the past:

> She **could** not move.

It can also refer to possibility in the future:

> Mind you, I s'pose I **could** always return as a newt …

With *have* it can refer to possible past events:

> She **could** not have failed to hear them.

countable noun

A noun that has both a SINGULAR and a PLURAL form. Most nouns are countable, because they refer to things that can be counted. A small number of nouns do not regularly have a plural form and are called UNCOUNTABLE.

---

countable and uncountable nouns

There are certain words which can only be used with countable nouns and not with uncountables. Other words can only be used with uncountables and not with countables.

WORDS	COUNTABLE	UNCOUNTABLE	EXAMPLE
little, less, least	✗	✓	little sustenance
few, fewer	✓	✗	few children
much	✗	✓	much food
many several	✓	✗	many surprises

Some English speakers use *less* with countable nouns:

> Sent off **no less than 20 times** in his career, Johnson is a surprisingly quiet and tender man.

This is not standard English and should be avoided in formal situations, especially in writing.

dare

A verb that can be used as a normal verb and also as a MODAL AUXILIARY VERB. For this reason it is sometimes described as a 'semi-modal' verb. As a normal verb it is followed by the INFINITIVE form of the verb:

He **dared** to criticize the leader outright.

As a modal auxiliary verb it is followed by the verb stem:

But I **dare** say you like apples.

She **dared** not complain.

It can also stand alone in expressions such as:

Don't you **dare**!

dash

A punctuation mark that looks like an extended HYPHEN. It comes in two sizes, an em dash (—) and an en dash (-).

An em dash is used to mark a break in sentences:

■ It can be used in pairs to show words in PARENTHESIS:

In brute material terms he was an accomplice—in fact, a conspirator—to the murder of millions of children.

■ It can introduce something that develops, or is an example of, what has gone before:

You must have seen it, I am sure — the blue flag with a white square in the middle.

■ In more formal writing, a COLON would be used instead of a dash.

■ It can introduce an aside by the writer:

I occupied Piers' old studio and Toby the three guest rooms — this purely for company.

■ In direct speech it can show that someone breaks off in mid sentence, or is interrupted:

I smiled and she said, 'You mean you want me to — ?

An en dash is used to show sequences:

1999–2000
an A–Z guide.

In sequences either use *from 1999 to 2000* or *1999–2000*; mixing the two styles, e.g. *from 1999–2000*, is wrong.

determiner

A class of words that forms an important part of many NOUN PHRASES. The determiner comes before the noun and helps to define it. Common determiners are:

a	an	the				
this	that	these	those			
some	any	no				
my	our	your	his	her	its	their
many	few	little	much			
other	last	next				
one	two	three	etc.			
first	second	third	etc.			
all	both					
half	third	etc.				

dialect

A version of a language spoken in a particular geographical area or by a particular group of people. The English spoken in Newcastle is different from that spoken by natives of North Cornwall. Not only do speakers in these two areas have a different **accent**, they also use a number of different words. Different dialects also use slightly different grammar, too. For example, in Devon some people say 'They do have ...' in preference to 'They have ...' Such regional expressions are not 'wrong', they simply differ from STANDARD ENGLISH. They are sometime described as 'non-standard'.

digraph

Two letters written together to represent a single sound. For example, these are consonant digraphs:

ch   ck   gh   ph   sh   th

There are also many vowel digraphs in English. For example:

ai   au   ea   ei   oa   oi   ou

For historical reasons, the letters 'a' and 'e' are frequently joined in the older spelling of words such as *medieval*:

mediæval

The use of this digraph is, however, dying out.

diminutive

■ A version of a noun that refers to a small version of something. Such diminutives are formed by adding a PREFIX:

minibus   microskirt

or a SUFFIX:

notelet   kitchenette   duckling

■ A version of a noun that indicates familiarity or fondness, formed by adding a suffix:

Aussie   sweetie   footer   champers

■ A short form of a personal name:

Timothy → Tim   Katherine → Kath/Kate/Katy

diphthong

A vowel sound that is composed of a sequence of two vowels. The vowel in the word 'so', for example begins with the 'o' sound of 'hot' and then glides into the 'u' sound of 'put'. Other diphthongs are the vowel sounds in the following words:

high   late   toil

Diphthongs should not be confused with DIGRAPHS.

direct object

See INDIRECT OBJECT.

direct speech

In stories, reports, and certain other types of writing, the words spoken by people can be reported (in REPORTED SPEECH) or quoted directly. Direct speech uses a set of punctuation conventions to separate the words actually spoken from the rest of the text, so that the reader does not get confused. The need for these 'rules' can be seen when we remove the punctuation from a piece of direct speech:

▶

He's very clever, you know. Very said Mr Datchery without enthusiasm. I mean, he's got a terrific lot of degrees and he's lived in all sorts of countries. So I guessed. There was a pause; then: but you *didn't* think he was clever, did you?

It is very difficult to follow what is going on. This is the same text with the direct speech correctly punctuated:

'He's very clever, you know.'

'Very,' said Mr Datchery without enthusiasm.

'I mean, he's got a terrific lot of degrees and he's lived in all sorts of countries.'

'So I guessed.'

There was a pause; then: 'But you *didn't* think he was clever, did you?'

Standard rules

- The words spoken are enclosed between inverted commas:

    'He's very clever, you know.'

  or

    "He's very clever, you know."

- If you normally use single inverted commas, then use double inverted commas for 'quotes within quotes':

    Then she said, 'I did it because Henry said, "I don't care what you do".'

  and vice versa:

    Then she said, "I did it because Henry said, 'I don't care what you do'."

- Every time there is a new speaker, start a new paragraph:

    'He's very clever, you know.'

    'Very,' said Mr Datchery without enthusiasm.

- Each new piece of speech begins with a capital letter, even if it is not at the beginning of the sentence:

    There was a pause; then: 'But you *didn't* think he was clever, did you?'

▶

- Each piece of speech should be preceded by a comma or colon:

  There was a pause; then: 'But you *didn't* think he was clever, did you?'

- There should normally be a comma, full stop, question mark, or exclamation mark at the end of a piece of speech. This is generally placed *before* the closing inverted comma(s):

  'He's very clever, you know.'

  'Very,' said Mr Datchery without enthusiasm.

- If the piece of speech is interrupted or the speaker trails off, then it can be ended with a dash or three dots:

  'I shall, thank you. Is there anything — '

  'Anything new? No, nothing.'

disjunct

A SENTENCE ADVERBIAL that provides some comment by the speaker or writer on the content of the sentence in which they appear. Disjuncts often come at or near the beginning of the sentence. In the sentences that follow the disjuncts are printed in bold:

Admittedly, the enemy on this occasion was not Napoleon.

Fortunately, this year's monsoon was short but sharp, and improved water management has produced good floods.

The choice of wine he is, **wisely**, leaving to the club.

Common disjuncts include:

actually	admittedly	basically	briefly	clearly
frankly	in general	obviously	perhaps	personally
possibly	presumably	remarkably	roughly	(un)fortunately

do

An AUXILIARY VERB. Like *be* and *have*, *do* can be used both as an auxiliary and as a main verb. It is a common and useful main verb in sentences such as:

Overcoats will **do** more than keep you warm this winter.

Citröen has **done** a lot of work in this area, starting back with the BX.

Another assassin is waiting to **do** him in.

As an auxiliary verb it is used:

■ to make negative statements:

Water lilies **do not grow** well if water is falling on to their leaves.

■ to form questions:

'**Do you understand** me?' he asked a second time.

■ to form TAG QUESTIONS:

Well, it doesn't matter about anyone else, **does it**?

They didn't act like police, **did they**?

■ for emphasis:

And he **does like** to travel.

■ to avoid repetition:

I think you all know him better than **I do**.

either ... or ...

When these two conjunctions are used as a pair, the two expressions that are linked should be of the same grammatical status:

■ two words:

Neither of us feels compelled to get wed on **either moral or religious** grounds.

■ two phrases:

The money will help fund a resources library and make learning units available to small, remote groups **either on loan or as permanent gifts**.

■ two clauses:

It should quash the conviction and **either enter a verdict of acquittal or order a new trial**.

ellipsis

The omission of one or more words in order to avoid repetition. It is often done by replacing a complete verb phrase by an AUXILIARY VERB. Other clause components can also be omitted. Ellipsis is frequently used:

■ with contrasting subjects, objects, or adverbials:

> **You've** got more use for it than **I have**.

instead of

> You've got more use for it than I have use for it.

■ with the verbs *be* and *have*:

> I was sure it would be worth the effort of breaking them in — and it **was**.

instead of

> I was sure it would be worth the effort of breaking them in — and it was worth the effort of breaking them in.

■ with modal auxiliary verbs like *should* or *could*:

> Two of them disappeared without trace as fast as they **could**.

instead of

> Two of them disappeared without trace as fast as they could disappear without trace.

etymology

The study of the history of words, or the history of a particular word. Dictionaries often provide information about the etymology of words. For example:

> **ramekin**
> ▷ *noun* a small dish for baking and serving an individual portion of food.
> – ORIGIN mid 17th cent.: from French *ramequin*, of Low German or Dutch origin; compare with obsolete Flemish *rameken* 'toasted bread'.

exclamation

A remark expressing surprise, delight, pain, anger, or other strong emotion, often spoken with extra force or emphasis:

How wonderful!

In writing, exclamations are often shown by the use of an EXCLAMATION MARK. Exclamation sentences can have a special grammatical construction, which involves changing the normal sentence order and starting the sentence in one of two ways:

■ The sentence begins with *how* + ADJECTIVE:

How strange it looked from below!

(instead of *It looked strange from below.*)

■ The sentence begins with *what* + NOUN PHRASE:

What an incredible confidence trick the election polls have turned out to be.

(instead of *The election polls have turned out to be an incredible confidence trick.*)

In speech particularly, exclamations frequently contain no verb:

How stupid of me!

exclamation mark

The main use of the exclamation mark is to end sentences that express:

■ an exclamation:

'With a fixed bayonet! A fixed bayonet!' he repeated incredulously.

■ direct speech spoken loudly or shouted:

'The first one ... the first!' everybody yelled.

■ something that the writer or speaker finds amusing:

Her son was the biggest poacher — he was a devil: he'd rob your house in the middle of the day and let you see him!

It can also be used in brackets after a statement that the writer finds amusing or ironic:

I look ruddy, muscly, well covered (!), and just, shall we say, solid.

fewer or less?

In formal writing and speech, *fewer* should be used with COUNTABLE NOUNS and *less* with UNCOUNTABLE NOUNS. Examples:

Fewer shades of green.

Parliament would have less power.

It is not standard English to use *less* with a plural or a number higher than one, as in the following example:

Less people vote in Euro elections than vote in local elections.

See also COUNTABLE AND UNCOUNTABLE NOUNS.

finite clause

A clause that contains a FINITE VERB.

finite verb

A form of the VERB that is complete in itself and can be used alone as the VERB PHRASE in a sentence. In the sentences that follow there is one finite verb, which is printed in bold type:

Then I **examined** the three main rooms.

Science **tells** us about the structural and relational properties of objects.

The finite form of the verb is either the SIMPLE PAST TENSE (as in the first example) or the SIMPLE PRESENT TENSE (as in the second example). The sentences that follow do not contain finite verbs; the verbs in bold type are non-finite:

Habit of **appearing to stand** on tiptoe, **stretching** the neck.

So kitsch, **frozen** in time.

If the verb phrase in a sentence consists of more than one verb word, then one of the verbs should be finite. In the sentences that follow, the verb phrase is printed in italics and the finite verb is in bold:

Magazine editors in 1955 *were hit* by the same problem.

The jazz scene *must have sounded* to Parker like a musical hall of mirrors.

first person

The PERSONAL PRONOUNS *I* and *we* are referred to as first person singular and first person plural respectively. When a story or report is written using the pronoun *I* it is said to be written in the first person, or to be a first-person narrative:

> I then went off for lunch, which was soup and crayfish.

focus

Some ADVERBIALS are used to focus attention on one part of a sentence:

> Paul regularly runs out of the nursery to play ball in a busy street; he has **also** run home by himself and was nearly hit by a lorry.

The writer is adding to the dangerous things that Paul has done, and the adverb *also* helps focus our attention. If we remove the word, the sentence is much weaker:

> Paul regularly runs out of the nursery to play ball in a busy street; he has run home by himself and was nearly hit by a lorry.

Other examples of sentences with focusing adverbials are:

> Utah, **in particular**, needs all the new employers it can find.

> **Only** the flowers in the vase on the table in front of me seemed real.

full stop

Full stops are used:

■ to mark the end of a sentence:

> And then you put it in the mail, and you repeat this process *ad infinitum* until the damn thing sells.

■ to mark the end of a group of words that is not a full sentence, but which is complete in itself:

> Over and over. Again and again. Relentlessly.

■ after abbreviations that consist of the first part of a word:

> Sept.   Thurs.

■ in email and website addresses:

> www.oup.com.

future continuous tense

A tense formed by *will be* or *shall be* followed by the PRESENT PARTICIPLE:

I shall be working.

Uses

To describe a future action, but emphasizing that it will go on over a period of time:

I **shall be working** quite late tonight.

To refer to planned or arranged events in the future:

Mr Wilkins **will be working** at the library during the next year.

To make promises or threats:

I **will be making** an announcement to the audience before the curtain rises.

future perfect continuous tense

The tense used to describe an action that will have been completed at a particular point in the future. It emphasizes that the action will have been going on over a period of time:

Some readers **will have been growing** roses for years.

future perfect tense

A tense formed by *will have* or *shall have* followed by the PAST PARTICIPLE:

She will have worked.

Uses

To predict that a future action will be finished by a particular time:

Key staff **will have completed** CC1 and CC2 training by April 1993.

To make deductions:

Jennifer **will have had** enough by now.

We're sure club members **will have worked** very hard to make this event a great success.

grading adjectives

MODIFYING an adjective by placing one or more adverbs in font of it. For example:

a beautiful view

a **rather** beautiful tropical garden

extremely beautiful drawings

Only QUALITATIVE ADJECTIVES can be graded. CLASSIFYING ADJEC-TIVES cannot normally be graded.

grapheme

A term from linguistics meaning the smallest unit in writing that can change meaning. In practice this means:

- a letter
- a punctuation mark

g

he, she, or it?

In English there isn't a pronoun that can refer to a person without defining whether that person is male or female. This raises the problem of how to avoid choosing between *he* and *she* in sentences like this:

If your employee is over pension age, — ? — pays no employee's NI contributions.

There are a number of possible solutions:

- Use *he* throughout and apologize to the reader, explaining that you mean *he* or *she*. Alternatively, use *she* throughout with a similar gloss:

If your employee is over pension age, **he** pays no employee's NI contributions.

If your employee is over pension age, **she** pays no employee's NI contributions.

Many people find this approach unacceptable.

- Use *he or she* (or *him or her*) throughout:

▶

If your employee is over pension age, **he or she** pays no employee's NI contributions.

This is generally acceptable but can be rather long-winded and clumsy, especially if used a lot.

■ Turn the sentence into the plural:

If your **employees are** over pension age, **they pay** no employee's NI contributions.

This is both acceptable and neat, but sometimes it is not possible.

■ Use the pronouns *they/them*, even though the noun they refer to is singular:

If your employee is over pension age, **they pay** no employee's NI contributions.

This is increasingly used, but traditionalists disapprove because they consider it ungrammatical. For this reason it should be avoided in more formal writing.

■ Turn the sentence into the passive:

No employee's NI contributions need be paid by employees over pension age.

This is often a neat solution, provided that the sentence isn't too long and doesn't become difficult to understand.

hers/her's

Hers is a POSSESSIVE PRONOUN which is used in sentences such as:

He put his hand in **hers**.

Her's is not standard English.

homograph

Two words which are written in the same way but which are pronounced differently and have different meanings. An example is *sow*, which can mean to put seeds in the ground, but when pronounced differently refers to a female pig.

See also HOMONYM.

homonym

Two (or more) words which look or sound the same, but have distinct and unrelated meanings. These fall into three groups:

■ Words which are written and pronounced in the same way:

seal   tackle   last   swallow

■ Words which are written in the same way but pronounced differently:

sow   lead

These are also referred to as HOMOGRAPHS.

■ Words which sound the same but are written differently:

meet/meat   right/write/rite

These are also referred to as HOMOPHONES.

homophone

Two (or more) words which sound the same but which are written differently. For example;

meet/meat/mete   right/write/rite

See also HOMONYM.

how

An ADVERB with four main uses:

■ To introduce a QUESTION:

How are you feeling?

■ To introduce a NOUN CLAUSE:

This is **how** they did it.

■ With an ADJECTIVE or another adverb:

You have no idea **how** heavy flowers can be.

He had noticed before **how** slowly the British matured.

■ To introduce an EXCLAMATION:

How remarkable!

however

An ADVERB with two main uses:

■ To MODIFY an ADJECTIVE or another adverb:

> We cannot afford to postpone necessary actions, **however** difficult, in the future.

■ As a SENTENCE ADVERBIAL or CONJUNCT:

> There was, **however**, one important difference.

This is the traditional way to use the word, enclosed between commas, as here. It can also be placed at the beginning of the sentence:

> **However**, they may not need a bus much longer.

hyphen

A punctuation mark with three uses:

Spelling

Some COMPOUND WORDS are linked by a hyphen. There is no simple rule to help know which compounds need hyphens and which do not. Hyphens are, however, being used less and less, especially in compound nouns. People tend to write *website* rather than *web-site*, and *air raid* instead of *air-raid*. Hyphens are still often used:

■ to form a verb from a compound noun:

> **a booby trap**
>
> The area was heavily mined and **booby-trapped**.

■ to form a noun from a phrasal verb or prepositional verb:

> I don't want you to **build up** your hopes and then be let down.
>
> a **build-up** of harmful gases

■ to form a word with a prefix:

> co-opt   multi-storey   post-war

■ to form some compound adjectives:

> easy-care   head-on   right-handed

Don't use a hyphen between the two parts of a phrasal verb:

> Time to **top up** your mobile phone.

Sentence construction (SYNTAX)

Sometimes it is important to show that certain words in a sentence are meant to be read together. If the hyphen or hyphens were not used, the meaning might not be clear. Compare these two sentences:

I wonder if he's thought of a **ready-to-wear** collection.

Our quality clothes are **ready to wear**.

A hyphen is often used when a two-word compound is placed before a noun to MODIFY it:

The destruction caused by mink is **well known**.

The son of a **well-known** actor.

Printing

Hyphens are also used in printed texts to split words that will not fit on to the end of a line. There are rules about how words should be split, which can be found in some dictionaries. Many computer word-processing and desktop publishing programmes offer automatic and manual hyphenation.

I/me

I is the SUBJECTIVE form and *me* is the OBJECTIVE form of the PERSONAL PRONOUN.

■ The **subjective form** should be used for the SUBJECT of a sentence:

My husband and I own six dogs.

In formal language it should also be used for the SUBJECT COMPLEMENT:

It is I who am wrong, not you.

Increasingly in less formal language *me* is used in such sentences:

Come on, this is **me**, remember?

■ The **objective form** should be used for the OBJECT of a sentence:

▶

For all I know you've manipulated both William Ash and **me** into this whole situation!

It is also used after a preposition:

Which is how it was **with** my husband and **me**.

■ In some DIALECTS *me* is used as the subject of the verb:

Cos **me** and him **are** good friends, like.

This is not STANDARD ENGLISH and some speakers work so hard to avoid it that they use *I* when they should use *me*. For example:

This is just another publishing trick to **make** you and I talk about it — which we are.

In this sentence the pronoun is the object of the verb *make* and so it should be *me*:

This is just another publishing trick to **make** you and **me** talk about it — which we are.

The commonest example of this use of *I* instead of *me* is the expression *between you and I/me*. Since the pronoun is preceded by a PREPOSITION, it should, of course, be *me*.

if

A SUBORDINATING CONJUNCTION used to introduce conditional clauses (see CONDITION).

It can also be used:

■ with *what* to form questions about things that might happen in the future or might have happened in the past:

What if I find certain issues or situations difficult?

What if he had become much more ruthless in that time?

■ to MODIFY an ADJECTIVE or ADVERB:

It was a delicious, **if** small, compensation.

Trade unions began, **if** slowly and unadventurously, to assert that they didn't give a hoot.

imperative

The imperative is the form of the verb used to make commands:

'Go away!' cried Mary.

It consists of the STEM of the verb. Imperative CLAUSES have a special form. They resemble a normal clause, but there is no SUBJECT. In effect the subject is *you*, but it is not stated:

'(You) go away!' cried Mary.

indirect object

Certain TRANSITIVE verbs can have two objects:

■ a direct object
■ an indirect object

For example:

We	gave	them	an early Christmas present.
She	told	me	the story.
SUBJECT	VERB	INDIRECT OBJECT	DIRECT OBJECT

As the examples show, the two types of object convey a different meaning. The indirect object tells us about the person or thing that benefits from the action described by the verb: *they* received the early Christmas present; *I* heard the story.

Verbs which commonly have an indirect object as well as a direct one include:

| bring | buy | give | promise |
| send | show | teach | tell |

infinitive

A form of the VERB. In the VERB PHRASE the infinitive has two forms:

■ the verb STEM. This form of the infinitive is used after MODAL AUXILIARY VERBS such as *must* and *should*:

| Life | must | | go | on. |
| | MODAL AUXILIARY | | INFINITIVE | |

■ 'to' plus the verb stem:

I	would	like	to meet	these people.
	VERB	VERB	INFINITIVE	

infinitive clause

A clause in which the verb is not a FINITE VERB, but an INFINITIVE.
The following examples show the similarities and differences
between the two types of clause:

TYPE OF CLAUSE	FINITE CLAUSE	INFINITIVE CLAUSE
Noun	I want **what is best for my little girl.**	All I really want is **to have a home of my own.**
Relative	And that was another thing **that was troubling her.**	There was only one thing **to do** in these circumstances.
Adverbial	Physiotherapy is important **so that hands, arms, legs, etc. are kept mobile.**	I need a couple more calls **to finish off the programme.**

inflection

Most NOUNS and VERBS and many ADJECTIVES change their form
according to how they are used in a sentence. This process is
called inflection.

■ Nouns inflect to show the plural:

one car → several car**s**

one child → several child**ren**

■ Some adjectives inflect to make the COMPARATIVE and SUPERLATIVE
forms:

tall → tall**er** → tall**est**

■ Verbs inflect to show NUMBER and PERSON in the present tense:

I work → she work**s**

- They also inflect to show the difference between past and present tenses:

    I work → I work**ed**

    I write → I **wrote**

- There are also inflections to form the PRESENT PARTICIPLE:

    write → writ**ing**

- and the past participle:

    write → writ**ten**

initialism

See ACRONYM

intensifier

An ADVERB that is used to MODIFY an ADJECTIVE. Intensifiers show how much of a quality something has. For example:

a beautiful view

a **rather** beautiful tropical garden

extremely beautiful drawings

Intensifiers can also modify other adverbs. For example:

easily

fairly easily

incredibly easily

interrogative clause

The type of clause used to ask QUESTIONS.

Yes/no questions

For questions expecting the answer *yes* or *no* the form of the verb and the word order are changed:

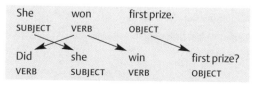

Question-word questions

These are introduced by a question word. The verb form and word order are different from those in a statement sentence:

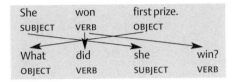

See also QUESTIONS.

intransitive verb

A VERB that does not have to be followed by an OBJECT. For example:

groan: The man on the terrace was groaning.

laugh: We both laughed.

Some verbs can be either TRANSITIVE or intransitive. For example, **write**:

Why hadn't Ken told him he was writing?

She was writing an essay.

inverted commas

Punctuation marks used to separate a group of words from the rest of the text. They can be single:

'and'

or double:

"and"

They are used as follows:

Direct speech

'He's very clever, you know.'

'Very,' said Mr Datchery without enthusiasm.

See also DIRECT SPEECH.

Titles

In handwritten documents and in some printed texts, they are used for the titles of books, pictures, plays, films, and TV programmes:

> 'The Taming of the Shrew'

> 'On the Waterfront'

Frequently, however, titles are shown in print by the use of italics.

Quotations

When a text includes a direct quotation from another book, or from what someone has said, quotation marks are used to mark it off:

> Alan Lomax calls the work song a 'spiritual speed-up'.

But if the passage to be quoted is fairly long it is often set out differently on the page, usually by indenting:

> The African musicologist Nicholas Ballanta-Taylor describes it:

>> Music in Africa is not cultivated for its own sake. It is always used in connection with dances or to accompany workmen. The rhythmic interest of the songs impels them to work and takes away the feeling of drudgery ...

When this is done, inverted commas are not necessary.

'Not my idea'

A similar use is when writers want to make it clear that an expression is not their own or one that they would choose:

> Many larger houses were being split up into so-called 'flats'.

In this example the use of *so-called* signals the writer's feeling, but the inverted commas will do the job on their own:

> Many larger houses were being split up into 'flats'.

Single or double?

There is no fixed rule about whether to use single or double inverted commas. The following guidelines should, however, be followed:

■ Choose either single or double and use them consistently. Single inverted commas tend to be preferred in Britain and double in the US.

■ If you need to include a quotation within a quotation, enclose it in the type of inverted commas you have not yet used. So if you normally use single inverted commas, put an enclosed quotation in double, and vice versa:

> 'He wondered if that was what was before them, but did not say anything. Best not to know. "The story has to be finished, and I must be the one to finish it." The words were like stones in his mouth.'

or

> "He wondered if that was what was before them, but did not say anything. Best not to know. 'The story has to be finished, and I must be the one to finish it.' The words were like stones in his mouth."

irregular verb

A verb that does not form its PAST TENSE and PAST PARTICIPLE in a regular way. Regular verbs work like this:

STEM	PAST TENSE	PAST PARTICIPLE
happen	happened	happened
tango	tangoed	tangoed
smile	smiled	smiled

If the stem ends in a consonant or a vowel other than *e*, then you add the letters *ed*. If the stem ends in *e* then the letter *d* is added.

Irregular verbs do not follow this pattern. Linguists divide them into seven different groups within which there are patterns. For everyday purposes it is more helpful to divide them into three:

■ Verbs in which the stem, the past tense, and the past participle each have a different form.

■ Verbs in which the past tense and the past participle have the same form which is different from the stem.

■ Verbs where all three are the same.

GROUP	STEM	PAST TENSE	PAST PARTICIPLE
1	take	took	taken
	swim	swam	swum
2	swing	swung	swung
	bind	bound	bound
3	hit	hit	hit
	burst	burst	burst

There are two verbs which are even more irregular: *be* and *go*:

STEM	PRESENT TENSE	PAST TENSE	PAST PARTICIPLE
be	is/am/are	was/were	been
go	go/goes	went	gone

is/are

VERBS have different forms in the SIMPLE PRESENT TENSE depending on the NUMBER and PERSON of the SUBJECT. For the verb *be* these are:

	SINGULAR	PLURAL
1ST PERSON	I am	we are
2ND PERSON	you are (thou art)	you are
3RD PERSON	he/she/it is	they are

It also has different forms in the SIMPLE PAST TENSE:

	SINGULAR	PLURAL
1ST PERSON	I was	we were
2ND PERSON	you were (thou wert)	you were
3RD PERSON	he/she/it was	they were

It is important to make sure that subject and verb agree, and if the subject is a single NOUN or a short NOUN PHRASE there isn't usually a problem. In longer sentences, especially where the subject is an extended noun phrase, difficulties can some-times arise. For example:

▶

Administrative blunders and a four-year delay in settling the dispute **was** described yesterday as a scandal by union leaders involved in the battle.

The subject of the sentence is *Administrative blunders and a four-year delay in settling the dispute*. This is formed of two noun phrases joined by *and*:

Administrative blunders	**and**	a four-year delay in settling the dispute

So it **must** be plural not singular and the verb should be *were*. In the sentence that follows the error has a different cause:

Israel's five hours of talks with Syria, which started on Sunday after much diplomatic wrangling, **was** described as frustrating.

Here the writer has made the verb agree with the noun phrase that is nearest to it: *much diplomatic wrangling*. In fact the subject is:

Israel's five hours of talks with Syria, which started on Sunday after much diplomatic wrangling

To be sure of the correct form of the verb it is necessary to identify the HEADWORD of the NOUN PHRASE — the word that lies at its heart. What was the person who described this talking about when he said that it was 'frustrating'? The answer has to be 'the talks'. And as *talks* is plural, the verb must be plural too, so it should be *were*.

it + passive

In formal writing it is quite common to begin a sentence with *it* followed by the PASSIVE form of the VERB. For example:

It is felt that a person propelling a motorcycle with his legs astride the cycle and his feet on the ground by 'paddling' it, would be driving.

The sentence is taken from a legal text, so it needs to be precise. 'It is felt' is imprecise because it is unclear who it refers to. (And *felt* is rather a vague term.) Better to say:

> If someone sits astride a motor cycle and uses their feet to 'paddle' it along the ground, then, in law, they are driving.

See also ACTIVE OR PASSIVE?

its/it's

This is an occasion where the use of the apostrophe can cause problems. The rule is as follows:

its

This is the POSSESSIVE form:

> His face had lost its boyish roundness.

it's

This is the short form of *it is*:

> It's a sign of growing up.

just

This adverb has two meanings:

■ a short time ago:

> He and his wife have just arrived here.

■ only:

> I just had time to see my mother and sister off.

Sometimes it is not clear which of the two meanings is intended:

> I've just bought this little flask.

Does this mean that the speaker **only** bought the flask and nothing else? Or that the speaker has bought it **very recently**? If you wish to be absolutely precise you may have to replace *just*, and/or add other words:

> I only bought this little flask — nothing else.

> I bought this little flask just now.

lexis

Another word for vocabulary: all the words that are used in a language, or a DIALECT of a language.

like/as/as if

Like is used as a PREPOSITION to show similarity between things:

> Was it that he looked so much **like** his father?

In informal speech and writing it is also used as a PREPOSITION in sentences such as:

> He looks **like** he's never seen an iron.

Purists frown on this use of *like* and consider it 'uneducated' even though this usage dates back at least as far as Shakespeare. (Darwin, for example, wrote, 'Unfortunately few have observed like you have done.') If you wish to avoid this kind of criticism, in formal writing and speech use *as* or *as if*:

> He looks **as if** he's never seen an iron.

> Unfortunately few have observed **as** you have done.

linking verb

MAIN VERBS can be divided into:

■ TRANSITIVE

■ INTRANSITIVE

■ LINKING

Linking verbs are used in sentences such as:

SUBJECT	LINKING VERB	COMPLEMENT
All the rumours	were	true
That	seems	healthy

By far the commonest linking verb is *be*. Others are:

> seem   appear   become   look

lists and punctuation

It is quite common to include lists of items in a piece of continuous prose. Punctuation has two purposes in presenting such lists:

1. To separate the items in the list.
   This is normally done by placing a COMMA after each item:

   > He had come equipped with a bottle of white wine, pâté, French bread, and fruit.

   If each item in the list is quite long, semicolons are sometimes used instead of commas:

   > Weeds may reach the lawn in various ways: as seeds blown by the wind; carried by birds; brought in on muddy footwear, machinery, or tools; or concealed in unsterilized soil or badly made compost used for top dressing.

2. To introduce the list.
   If the list itself is not particularly long, there is no need to use any punctuation to introduce it:

   > He had come equipped with a bottle of white wine, pâté, French bread, and fruit.

   Longer lists, especially in formal writing, can be introduced by a COLON:

   > Weeds may reach the lawn in various ways: as seeds blown by the wind ...

   This can also be done less formally by a DASH:

   > It contained quite a bit of information — the position of the police telephones, the infirmaries, the hospitals, fire brigade, fire boxes, and so on.

Comma before 'and'?

The last item in a list is usually preceded by *and*. Some writers and publishers always place a comma before this *and*:

> In fact, English criminal law has a wide range of such offences, of which those involving firearms, offensive

▶

> weapons, motor vehicles, and other endangerment will be
> outlined here.
>
> Other writers do not. This partly a question of individual style.
> But the comma before *and* is sometimes necessary. Two items
> joined by *and* can appear to belong together. If you read the
> sentence that follows without much care it may seem rather
> strange:
>
> > Other sources of calcium if milk does not agree with you
> > are yoghurt, cheese, shrimps and ice cream.
>
> 'Shrimps and ice cream'? A comma would avoid any such
> momentary confusion:
>
> > Other sources of calcium if milk does not agree with you
> > are yoghurt, cheese, shrimps, and ice cream.

main clause

Every full SENTENCE contains at least one main clause. Sometimes
two (or more) main clauses are linked together using COORDIN-
ATING CONJUNCTIONS to form a COMPOUND SENTENCE:

MAIN CLAUSE	COORDINATING CONJUNCTION	MAIN CLAUSE
Aja knew everyone in town.		
My father-in-law had a great gift for friendship.		
No man can face this situation without uneasiness	and	these circumstances were exceptional.

The two clauses in the last example can be joined in other ways, by
making one of them dependent on the other: by turning it into a
subordinate clause:

MAIN CLAUSE	SUBORDINATING CONJUNCTION	SUBORDINATE CLAUSE
No man can face this situation without uneasiness	so	these circumstances were exceptional.

SUBORDINATING CONJUNCTION	SUBORDINATE CLAUSE	MAIN CLAUSE
Although	no man can face this situation without uneasiness	these circumstances were exceptional.

main verb

The VERB PHRASE in a CLAUSE can contain two types of VERB: main verbs and AUXILIARY verbs. If it only contains a single verb, then that is a main verb. If it contains more than one, then one will be a main verb and the other(s) auxiliary. In the examples that follow the **main verb** is in bold type and the *auxiliary verb(s)* in italics.

Strange men **moved** about the streets in pairs.

Everything now *was* always **reminding** me of something else.

By 1646 the Royalists *were* **defeated**.

In the second example above, the auxiliary verb is used to form the TENSE:

was reminding: past continuous tense

In the last example the auxiliary is used to form the PASSIVE VOICE.

manner

ADVERBIALS and ADVERBIAL CLAUSES can be used to provide information about **how** things occur.

Adverbials

In the sentences that follow, the adverbials are printed in bold type.

She drifted **slowly** over to the telephone.

The trees rushed past **at great speed**.

Adverbial clauses

Adverbial clauses of manner can be used in a similar way:

> She had arrived early, **as she always does**.

> Ted was a child of the sixties, but he sounded **as if he'd been born in the Blitz**.

It is also possible to have NON-FINITE CLAUSES of manner:

> He made **as if to get ready to leave**.

mass noun

See UNCOUNTABLE NOUN.

may

A MODAL AUXILIARY VERB with two meanings:

■ permission

> Thank you, Mrs Prynn, you **may** leave us now.

■ possibility

> They **may** come in handy.

See also CAN/MAY, MAY/MIGHT.

---

may/might

These two MODAL AUXILIARY VERBS are sometimes confused. They both refer to possible situations:

1 They may come in handy.

The situation is possible now and in the future. The speaker/writer can clearly imagine it taking place.

2 You might want to add to a set of chairs that you already possess.

The situation is possible now and in the future, but the speaker/writer is treating it as purely hypothetical — it could happen in the future but then so could a lot of other things.

3 Joe Burns lowered his voice, as if they might be overheard.

▶

The situation occurred in the past. At that time it was open and possible. If Joe Burns had spoken he would have said, '*We may be overheard.*'

4 It belonged to a Miss Angela Morgan, and you may have seen the death reported.

The sentence refers to a past event which was possible. The speaker/writer can clearly imagine it having occurred.

5 The seeds of life might have appeared spontaneously here or in space, or they might have been deliberately sent here by an extraterrestrial intelligence.

The sentence refers to past events which were possible. The speaker is talking about hypothetical events — any of them could be true, as could others.

These distinctions are now frequently ignored and it may be that at some point in the future they will cease to exist.

m

might

A MODAL AUXILIARY VERB used to indicate possibility.
See also MAY/MIGHT.

modal auxiliary verb

An AUXILIARY VERB is one that is used with a MAIN VERB to form a VERB PHRASE:

SUBJECT	MODAL AUXILIARY VERB	PRIMARY AUXILIARY VERB	MAIN VERB
She		has	taken
They	might		take
We	should	have	taken

The modal auxiliary verbs are:

shall	will	should	would
can	could		
may	might		
must			
ought (to)			

modal meanings

Modal auxiliary verbs can be used to convey a wide range of meanings. The table below illustrates some of the commonest, but it is by no means exhaustive.

MEANING	VERBS USED	EXAMPLE
Ability	can, could	I need interpreters in my surgery who **can** speak Punjabi, Urdu, and Gujarati.
Potential	can, could, might, ought to, should, will, would	A suitable satellite in high orbit **should** do it nicely.
Permission	can, could, may, might	Candidates **may** enter for both examinations, if desired.
Requests and invitations	can, could, may, might, will, would	**Will** you come with me?
Offers, promises, threats	can, could, shall, should	The Company **will** keep a copy of all material delivered to the Publisher.
Prediction	could, may, might, should, will	It **could** be dangerous for anybody who knows.

MEANING	VERBS USED	EXAMPLE
Obligation	must, ought to, should	No matter what else they do within the group, every volunteer **must** do at least one shift on the phones every fortnight.
Advice	could, might, must, ought to, should	'Perhaps you **could** try waders,' suggested Preston.
Habitual actions	might, will, would	Every afternoon she **would** wake from her afternoon sleep and cry pitifully, sometimes for as long as two hours.

m

modify/modifier

In grammar, to modify is to change or add to the meaning of another word. A modifier is a word or group of words that does this.

■ ADJECTIVES modify NOUNS.

■ NOUNS can also be modified by other NOUNS and by PREPOSITIONAL PHRASES.

In the examples that follow, the modifiers are printed in bold.

Edgar Degas favoured his studio to the **open** (adjective) air, preferring to paint at the racecourse and in **ballet** (noun) studios.

There was a smear **of mud** (prepositional phrase) on his nose.

■ ADVERBS modify ADJECTIVES.

Isabella can **very** (adverb) easily come across as a prig.

Modifiers that come before the word they modify are referred to as PREMODIFIERS:

open air

Those that follow the word they modify are POSTMODIFIERS:

    a smear **of mud**

See also NOUN PHRASE, ADJECTIVE PHRASE, ADVERB PHRASE.

morpheme

The lowest unit of language that can convey meaning. You cannot break a morpheme down into anything smaller that has a meaning. Many simple words are morphemes. For example:

    child   shed   walk

Some words consist of two or more morphemes:

    child+ren   child+ish

    walk+s   walk+ing

ren, *ish*, *s*, *ing* all convey some meaning, even though none of them is a word in its own right. If we try to break them down any further we just end up with letters or sounds:

    r+e+n   i+s+h

None of these conveys meaning on its own.

morphology

The study of how words are built up and how they change according to their use in sentences. With SYNTAX it forms the grammar of the language. This can be shown in the following sentence:

    Bharati's words gave him an idea.

Morphology tells us, for example, that the plural of the NOUN *word* is formed by adding the letter 's', and that the VERB *give* is IRREGULAR and its PAST TENSE is *gave*. Syntax tells us that the sentence is SIMPLE and is made up of a SUBJECT, VERB, INDIRECT OBJECT, and DIRECT OBJECT.

multiple sentence

A sentence that contains more than one FINITE CLAUSE. (As opposed to a SIMPLE SENTENCE that only contains one finite clause.) Multiple sentences are divided into COMPOUND SENTENCES and COMPLEX SENTENCES.

must

A MODAL AUXILIARY VERB used to express the speaker's view of how necessary or desirable an event may be:

'I must go,' breathed Stefania, and was gone.

See also MODAL MEANINGS.

neither ... nor ...

When these two conjunctions are used as a pair the two expressions that are linked should be of the same grammatical status:

■ two words:

Neither Squigs nor Goblins ever returned.

■ two phrases:

Our weather is **neither too hot nor too cold**.

■ two clauses:

... the plain man who questions **neither what he sees nor what he likes** ...

need

A verb that can be used as a normal MAIN VERB or as a MODAL AUXILIARY VERB. For this reason it is sometimes described as a 'semi-modal' verb.

As a main verb

It is a TRANSITIVE verb (one that requires an OBJECT):

They **needed** clothes that would not get torn in a fight.

As a modal auxiliary verb

It is followed by 'to' and the stem of a main verb:

They **needed to rest**, they said, but showed no signs of doing so.

In QUESTIONS and negative statements the 'to' is omitted:

Need I say more?

He need not have worried.

none are/none is

People sometimes say that you should always follow the PRONOUN *none* with a SINGULAR verb. They argue that *none is* is always correct and *none are* always wrong, because *none* is derived from *not one* so must always be singular. This is mistaken. Both are acceptable in educated speech and writing. In speech, and with phrases containing *none of*, a plural verb is more frequently used than a singular one. In writing, the situation is reversed. The best advice is to follow *none* with the form of the verb that makes best sense in the context:

1. Of the five bridges crossing the Tyne at Newcastle, **none is** more famous than the High Level Bridge.

2. There do not appear to have been any children (**none are** mentioned in his will).

In sentence 1 the writer implies that even if you examine the bridges **one by one** you won't find one that is more famous than the High Level Bridge. In sentence 2 the writer is concerned with *children* and so it makes sense to use the plural form of the verb.

n

non-finite clause

A structure which is used in the same way as a FINITE CLAUSE, but does not have a finite verb. Instead it has an infinitive, a present participle, or a past participle. In the examples that follow, the non-finite clause is in bold type and is followed in brackets by a finite version of the same structure.

■ INFINITIVE

You just don't know **when to stop**. (… when you should stop.)

■ PRESENT PARTICIPLE

Every person has a responsibility for maintaining safety **when travelling**. (… when they are travelling.)

■ PAST PARTICIPLE

They are cooled by water **taken from the River Yenisey**. (… which is taken from the River Yenisey.)

nor

A COORDINATING CONJUNCTION. It is often used as part of a pair: neither … nor ….

See also NEITHER … NOR …

noun

Nouns are words used to identify people, places, things, and ideas. As a grammatical class, nouns satisfy most or all of the following tests:

- NUMBER: they have a SINGULAR and a PLURAL form:

    one car, two cars   one child, several children

- DETERMINERS: they can be preceded by *a, an,* or *the*:

    a child   an apple   the cars

- MODIFIERS: they can be modified by an ADJECTIVE placed before them:

    a young child   a ripe apple   the new cars

- PHRASES: they can form the HEADWORD of a NOUN PHRASE:

    a ripe red apple ready to eat   the new cars on the forecourt

Nouns fall into a number of broad groups, each of which has a separate entry in this A–Z:

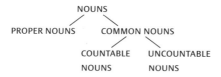

```
                      NOUNS
                     /      \
        PROPER NOUNS      COMMON NOUNS
                          /          \
                  COUNTABLE        UNCOUNTABLE
                  NOUNS            NOUNS
```

noun clause

A SUBORDINATE CLAUSE in a COMPLEX SENTENCE forming one of the following elements:

- SUBJECT

    What they want to do next is to use deuterium and tritium in the machine.

■ OBJECT

> We don't just let them do **what they want to do**.

■ SUBJECT COMPLEMENT

> This **what they want to do**.

■ OBJECT COMPLEMENT

> He made it **what it is today**.

A noun clause can also be the object of a PREPOSITION:

> Women make their own minds up **about what they want to do**.

noun phrase

A group of words built up round a single noun, which is called the HEADWORD of the phrase. The noun phrases that follow all have the same headword, *books*:

> books
>
> some books
>
> some books about photography
>
> some excellent books about photography
>
> some really excellent books about photography

Noun phrases can consist of the following parts:

DETERMINER	PREMODIFIER	HEADWORD	POSTMODIFIER
some	really excellent	books	about photography
a		visit	to the Sierra Maestra
the two	frothy	cups	of cappuccino

In clauses noun phrases can be:

■ SUBJECT

> **The hairy hand holding out the review to her** was insistent.

■ OBJECT

> Harry lifted **his bushy eyebrows** at Elizabeth.

■ SUBJECT COMPLEMENT

   It was **a stirring tune**.

■ OBJECT COMPLEMENT

   But now the party faithful have appointed him **crisis manager of a party still threatened by disintegration**.

■ part of a larger phrase, for example a PREPOSITIONAL PHRASE

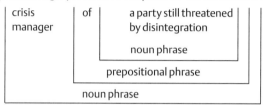

crisis manager	of	a party still threatened by disintegration
		noun phrase
	prepositional phrase	
noun phrase		

number

English grammar has two numbers, singular and plural. They are marked in the following ways:

Nouns

Most nouns have a singular and a plural form:

   house/houses   foot/feet

Pronouns

Many pronouns have a singular and plural form. For example:

SINGULAR	PLURAL
I	we
he/she/it	they
this	these

Verbs

In the third person of the SIMPLE PRESENT TENSE verbs have a different form for singular and plural:

SINGULAR	PLURAL
she walks	they walk

See also AGREEMENT.

object

In a statement the object:

- normally comes after the VERB
- is governed by the verb
- refers to a person, place, thing, or idea that is different from the SUBJECT
- often refers to a person, place, thing, or idea that is acted on or affected by the subject
- can be a noun, a pronoun, a noun phrase, or a noun clause:

REST OF SENTENCE	OBJECT	TYPE
She lost	consciousness.	NOUN
She lost	it.	PRONOUN
She lost	her libel case.	NOUN PHRASE
Most families lost	what was virtually their only source of income.	NOUN CLAUSE

See also INDIRECT OBJECT.

object complement

Part of a clause that completes the OBJECT. In statements it follows the object and refers to the same person, place, or thing:

SUBJECT	VERB	OBJECT	OBJECT COMPLEMENT
She	appointed	him	deputy party chairman

The object complement can be:

- a NOUN:

    I appointed him **skipper**.

- an ADJECTIVE or ADJECTIVE PHRASE:

    Cameron made him **uneasy**.

- a NOUN PHRASE:

    Both the ancient universities made him **an honorary doctor**.

- a NOUN CLAUSE:

    He made it **what it is today**.

objective case

See CASE.

omission marks

A number of dots, usually three, which are used to show that something has been missed out from a sentence. They have two main uses:

■ To reduce the length of a quotation, and/or to cut it down to its essentials:

> Endearing anecdotes about the great man follow, the sort that 'cling ... to all really great journalists'.

■ In DIRECT SPEECH to show that the speaker did not complete what he or she was saying:

> 'I really have to sit down.'
>
> 'Just see if you can go a little ...'
>
> Zero collapsed.

Some writers prefer to use a DASH for this purpose:

> 'I really have to sit down.'
>
> 'Just see if you can go a little — '
>
> Zero collapsed.

or

A COORDINATING CONJUNCTION often used as part of the pair *either ... or ...*.

ought

A MODAL AUXILIARY VERB used to refer to possible, rather than actual, events. It expresses a view about how desirable an action might be and is normally followed by the INFINITIVE of the main verb:

> You **ought to go and see** a doctor.

It can also stand alone:

> No, I **ought** not.

Negative

The negative form of verb phrases containing *ought* is formed simply by adding *not*: *you ought not to go and see the doctor*. It is not standard English to use *didn't ought to*.

paragraphs

Texts of any length written in continuous prose are usually divided into paragraphs. These are marked in print and writing by beginning a new line. There is usually also either a small gap between the paragraphs and/or the first line of a new paragraph is indented slightly.

Paragraphs are a useful way of helping the reader through a text. They are also useful to the writer in helping to give a text shape. Individual paragraphs usually have a typical pattern and are linked to each other in a variety of ways.

Example

Editing involves looking at the report and thinking about how it can be improved. Drafting, too, involves reading what you have written and thinking about how it can be improved. So what's the difference? It is a question of focus. When you draft you are thinking about yourself as writer: about what you want to communicate to your audience. When you edit, you think about your readers: you try to see things from their point of view.

It is important to understand this distinction, because unless you do, you will find it hard to edit what you have written. In many ways the person who wrote a text is the worst person to be given the job of editing it. They have been working at it for hours, days — months, even — and find it difficult to stand back from it and look at it objectively and dispassionately. That is exactly what an editor has to do, but it is something that the author finds very difficult to achieve. (That's why, when I have finished writing this book, I shall hand it over — with some relief — to a professional editor, who will look at it with fresh eyes.)

▸

Structure

A typical paragraph has three sections:

■ Lead sentence (sometimes called the topic sentence). This is normally the first or second sentence in the paragraph and tells the reader what the paragraph is about:

> Editing involves looking at the report and thinking about how it can be improved.

■ Body of the paragraph. There follow a number of sentences, usually between two and five, that develop this subject matter. In this case there are four which examine the similarities and differences between editing and drafting.

■ Concluding sentence. This has two purposes: to round off and/or sum up what has gone before, and to provide a lead in to the next paragraph.

In the case of the first paragraph in the example, the concluding sentence rounds off the 'argument' that editing is different from drafting:

> When you edit, you think about your readers: you try to see things from their point of view.

Links

If a text is to flow, the paragraphs need to be linked together. How this is done is explained in BUILDING TEXTS. Here the second paragraph begins with the words:

> It is important to understand this distinction, because unless you do, you will find it hard to edit what you have written.

The words *this distinction* refer back to the content of the previous paragraph. The whole sentence explains how this paragraph will develop the ideas of the previous one.

p

parenthesis

When something is put 'in parenthesis' it is separated off from the main part of the sentence by a pair of brackets, commas, or dashes. This is usually because it contains information or ideas that are not essential to an understanding of the sentence:

> With the homeless now crowding the streets of cities that once hardly knew them (like Portland, Oregon), Clinton has effectively criminalized the poor.

or because they form a comment by the author on the rest of the sentence:

> The poor, says Clinton (he means blacks and Hispanics), have been 'demotivated' by welfare and forced into a 'welfare' culture.

Brackets are the most formal (and most obvious) way of showing parenthesis:

> With the homeless now crowding the streets of cities that once hardly knew them (like Portland, Oregon), Clinton has effectively criminalized the poor.

Commas are less forceful:

> With the homeless now crowding the streets of cities that once hardly knew them, like Portland, Oregon, Clinton has effectively criminalized the poor.

Dashes are the least formal:

> With the homeless now crowding the streets of cities that once hardly knew them — like Portland, Oregon — Clinton has effectively criminalized the poor.

participle problems

A PRESENT PARTICIPLE can be used to form a NON-FINITE CLAUSE. If this is placed at the beginning of the sentence it should always refer to the SUBJECT of that sentence:

> **Having left Tony and his Mum at his appointment**, I set off in the direction of the motorway.

▶

Here the present perfect participle *having left* is attached to the subject of the sentence, *I*.

Sometimes writers forget this and begin a sentence with a participle that is not attached to anything stated in the sentence. The participle is said to be 'hanging' or 'dangling'. For example:

> Travelling to Finland, the weather got colder and colder. He wished he had brought more warm clothes with him.

Grammatically this means that the weather was travelling to Finland, whereas what the writer means is:

> As **he was** travelling to Finland, the weather got colder and colder ...

Good writing practice means avoiding 'hanging' or 'dangling' participles by making sure that the participle is attached to the subject of the sentence.

part of speech

The traditional name for what modern grammar refers to as a WORD CLASS. A group of words that have the same grammatical function.

passive voice

TRANSITIVE verbs can be used in two different ways, called VOICES: active and passive:

ACTIVE: A vicious Rottweiler dog attacked them.

PASSIVE: They were attacked by a vicious Rottweiler dog.

In the passive voice it is as if the object of the sentence gets a voice of its own and can describe an event from its own point of view. This applies even if the original subject is inanimate:

ACTIVE: A big wave hit the side of the paddle wheel.

PASSIVE: The side of the paddle wheel was hit by a big wave.

The transformation from active to passive works like this:

subject   active verb   object

subject   passive verb + *by*   agent

For example:

A vicious Rottweiler dog   attacked   them.

They   were attacked by   a vicious Rottweiler dog.

All the tenses that exist in the active voice can also occur in the passive, although some are rarely used:

	SIMPLE	CONTINUOUS	PERFECT	PERFECT CONTINUOUS
Past	I was hit	I was being hit	I had been hit	I had been being hit
Present	I am hit	I am being hit	I have been hit	I have been being hit
Future	I shall be hit	I shall be being hit	I shall have been hit	I shall have been being hit

See also ACTIVE OR PASSIVE?

p

past continuous tense

This tense is formed by *was* or *were* followed by the PRESENT PARTICIPLE of the MAIN VERB:

He was writing.

Uses

To show how one event occurred during another event:

While they **were talking**, they heard a terrific roar.

To refer to a completed event that went on over a period of time:

I **was working** there in 1933.

This tense is sometimes referred to as the 'imperfect' tense.

past participle

One of the forms of the VERB:

STEM	smile
INFINITIVE	to smile
PRESENT TENSE	smile/smiles
PRESENT PARTICIPLE	smiling
PAST TENSE	smiled
PAST PARTICIPLE	smiled

In regular verbs it is the same as the past tense form and is made by adding -ed to the verb stem (or just -d if the verb ends with the letter -e). In IRREGULAR VERBS it is formed in different ways.

The past participle is used to form a number of tenses:

■ PRESENT PERFECT: *I have smiled*

■ PAST PERFECT: *I had smiled*

■ FUTURE PERFECT: *I shall have smiled*

It is also used to form past tenses with MODAL AUXILIARIES (*I might have smiled, I should have smiled*, etc.).

past perfect continuous tense

This tense is formed by *had been* followed by the PRESENT PARTICIPLE:

She had been writing.

Uses

To refer to an action that continued over a period in the past:

He **had been studying** hard for some hours.

To refer to a continuing action in the past contrasted with a single completed action in the past:

Timothy Harris, 33, **had been working** in Ilfracombe, Devon, when he **met** his girlfriend Faye Whitehead.

past perfect tense

This tense is formed by *had* followed by the PAST PARTICIPLE:

She had written.

Uses

To refer to an action in the past that continues up to, or relates to, a single point in the past:

> By 1428 they **had established** a city state.

To contrast two events, one of which happened before the other:

> I went round after I **had finished**.

To show a causal link between two events in the past:

> She remembered because she **had seen** her drive off.

In narrative to give background information:

> It **had been** a bad year for Cliff.

past tense

See SIMPLE PAST TENSE.

person

PERSONAL PRONOUNS can be 1st, 2nd, or 3rd person, and singular or plural:

	SINGULAR	PLURAL
1st person	I	we
2nd person	you	you
3rd person	she, he, it	they

The person of the SUBJECT affects the form of the verb in the PRESENT TENSE (and in the PAST TENSE of the verb **be**):

	SINGULAR	PLURAL
1st person	I work	we work
2nd person	you work	you work
3rd person	she, he, it works	they work

This applies even if the actual personal pronoun is not used. For example:

> Mr and Mrs Hughes live …

See also NUMBER and AGREEMENT.

personal pronouns

A group of PRONOUNS that refer to people, things, or ideas. They have three CASES: SUBJECTIVE, OBJECTIVE, and POSSESSIVE:

	SUBJECTIVE		OBJECTIVE		POSSESSIVE	
	SINGULAR	PLURAL	SINGULAR	PLURAL	SINGULAR	PLURAL
1st person	I	we	me	us	mine	ours
2nd person	you	you	you	you	yours	yours
3rd person	she, he, it	they	her, him, it	them	hers, his, its	theirs

See also PRONOUN, POSSESSIVE CASE, POSSESSIVE PRONOUNS AND DETERMINERS.

phoneme

A speech sound. In speech as in writing we express ourselves using words. In writing each word is made up of letters, and in speech a word is made up of a series of phonemes. There are 44 phonemes in standard modern English, evenly divided between vowels and consonants. The phonemes in a word do not correspond to the letters with which we write it. For example, the word *catch* contains five letters: *c – a – t – c – h*, but only three sounds: *c – a – tch*.

phrasal verbs

A verb that consists of a MAIN VERB plus an ADVERB. Phrasal verbs can be TRANSITIVE or INTRANSITIVE. For example:

INTRANSITIVE	TRANSITIVE
back away	carry out
catch on	dig up
hold on	leave behind
settle down	spell out

Transitive phrasal verbs

The adverb can come before or after the object:

They've **dug up** a lot of human bones at my old uncle's house.

They've **dug** a lot of human bones **up** at my old uncle's house.

But if the object is a PERSONAL PRONOUN it normally comes before the adverb:

They should have **left** him **behind**.

If the object consists of a fairly long NOUN PHRASE, it is usually more convenient to place it after the adverb — otherwise the reader is left waiting for the completion of the verb. Compare these two versions of the same sentence:

Mr Lamont **spelled out** the tactics behind the battle for the pound.

Mr Lamont **spelled** the tactics behind the battle for the pound **out**.

See also PREPOSITIONAL VERBS.

phrase

A group of words that forms part of a CLAUSE. A phrase is built up on a HEADWORD, and the types of phrase are named according to the class the headword belongs to:

	HEADWORD	EXAMPLE	USES IN A CLAUSE
NOUN PHRASE	noun	a large **jug** of water	subject, object, complement
VERB PHRASE	verb	have been **seeing**	verb
PREPOSITIONAL PHRASE	preposition	**by** the roadside	adverbial, part of a noun phrase
ADJECTIVE PHRASE	adjective	very **big** indeed	part of a noun phrase, complement
ADVERB PHRASE	adverb	rather too **slowly**	adverbial

place

Adverbials and adverbial clauses can provide information about where something happened.

Adverbials

Adverbials of place can be individual words or prepositional phrases. In the examples that follow, the adverbials are printed in bold type.

> We should not have expected to see them **there**.

> A quarter of them live in **New York City**.

Adverbial clauses

These are usually introduced by the conjunctions:

> where   wherever   everywhere

For example:

> It just seems odd to do it **where no one is likely to see it**.

> **Wherever he went** things seemed different.

> **Everywhere one looked** there were unaccustomed trophies on display.

plural

See NUMBER.

P

possession

A term used in grammar to mean that something belongs to someone or something else.

■ With nouns we show possession by the use of the POSSESSIVE APOSTROPHE:

> Sue's bungalow

> The Government's admission

■ Pronouns change their form and can be used as POSSESSIVE PRONOUNS and POSSESSIVE DETERMINERS:

SUBJECTIVE PRONOUN	POSSESSIVE PRONOUN	POSSESSIVE DETERMINER
I	mine	my
she	hers	her
you	yours	your

possessive apostrophe

The APOSTROPHE is used to show that something belongs to someone. For example:

Lord Rochester's monkey

the girl's handbag

the Browns' Silver Wedding anniversary

the different churches' position on gay priests

As these examples show, the rule is that if the name or noun is in the singular, we add an apostrophe followed by the letter 's'. If the name or noun is a plural ending in 's' then we simply add an apostrophe. (Plurals that do not end in 's' follow the rule for singular nouns: *children's playground*.) There is one exception to the rule. When *its* means 'of it' there is no apostrophe.

possessive case

The possessive CASE of nouns is formed by using the POSSESSIVE APOSTROPHE. PERSONAL PRONOUNS have a possessive case which is shown in the table below.

SUBJECTIVE	POSSESSIVE
I	mine
we	ours
she	hers
he	his
it	its
you	yours
they	theirs

The pronoun *who* also has a possessive case: *whose*.

possessive pronouns and determiners

Personal pronouns have two possessive forms:

SUBJECTIVE FORM OF PRONOUN	POSSESSIVE PRONOUN	POSSESSIVE DETERMINER
I	mine	my
we	ours	our
she	hers	her
he	his	his
it	its	its
you	yours	your
they	theirs	their

Possessive pronouns are used on their own in a sentence. Possessive determiners always come before a noun:

> The manager has his problems but we have **ours** as well. (possessive pronoun)

> Fossils provide one of **our** most direct links with the prehistoric past. (possessive determiner)

prefix

Part of a word that comes before the BASE. Prefixes add to or alter the meaning of the base word in some way, as can be seen by the following examples.

BASE WORD	PREFIX	PRODUCT
market	super-	supermarket
	hyper-	hypermarket
interested	un-	uninterested
	dis-	disinterested

prefix meanings

PREFIX	MEANING	EXAMPLE
a-	not, not affected by	amoral
ante-	before	antecedent
anti-	against	anti-pollution
arch-	chief	arch-rival
auto-	self	autobiography
bi-	two	bipartisan
bio-	(from biology)	biodiversity
circum-	around	circumference
co-	joint, together	co-worker
contra-	opposite	contradiction
counter-	against	counteract
crypto-	hidden	crypto-fascist
de-	making the opposite of	demystify
demi-	half	demigod
di-	two	dialogue
dis-	making the opposite of	disagree
du-/duo-	two	duologue
eco-	(from ecology)	eco-tourism
Euro-	(from European)	Eurodollar
ex-	former	ex-husband
	out of	extract
fore-	in the front of, ahead of	forerunner
hyper-	very big	hypermarket
in-	not, opposite of	inexact
	in, into	insert
inter-	between	inter-state
intra-	inside	intravenous
mal-	bad(ly)	maladministration
mega-	very large	megastar
mid-	middle	midlife
midi-	medium-sized	midi-length
mini-	small	minimarket
mis-	wrong, false	misadventure
mono-	one	monogamy
multi-	many	multi-layered

p

PREFIX	MEANING	EXAMPLE
neo-	new	neolithic
non-	not, opposite of	non-partisan
out-	beyond	outreach
over-	too much	overreach
para-	ancillary	paramedic
	beyond	paranormal
poly-	many	polymath
post-	after	post-election
pre-	before	pre-election
pro-	for	pro-gun
	deputy	proconsul
pseudo-	false	pseudo-intellectual
re-	again	rerun
	back	reverse
retro-	backwards	retrograde
self-	self	self-sufficient
semi-	half	semi-serious
sub-	below	sub-zero
super-	more than, special	superhuman
supra-	above	suprasensuous
sur-	more than, beyond	surreal
tele-	at a distance	television
trans-	across	trans-Siberian
tri-	three	tripartite
ultra-	beyond	ultraviolet
	very much indeed	ultra-careful
un-	not, opposite of	unnecessary
	reversal, cancellation	untie
under-	below, less than	underachieve
uni-	one	unitary
vice-	deputy	vice-chancellor

P

preposition

A class of words used with nouns and other words to form
PREPOSITIONAL PHRASES. Prepositions form a small group of,
generally, small words. The commonest are:

about	above	across	after	against
along	among	around	as	at
before	behind	below	beneath	beside
between	beyond	but	by	despite
during	except	for	from	in
inside	into	like	near	of
off	on	over	past	round
since	through	throughout	till	to
towards	under	underneath	until	up
upon	with	within	without	

There are also two-, three-, and four-word prepositions:

along with	apart from	as well as	away from
because of	close to	except for	in front of
in the face of	instead of	next to	on to
on top of	out of	owing to	up to

Prepositions come before:

■ a NOUN:

below ground

■ a PRONOUN:

after me

■ a VERBAL NOUN:

without leaving

■ a NOUN PHRASE:

during the last month.

preposition at the end of a sentence

Some people argue that you should never place a preposition at the end of a sentence. They say that the word 'preposition' refers to something that is placed **before** ('pre-') something else, so it is absurd to place it last in the sentence where it cannot come before anything. This opinion is ingenious but completely wrong. Writers have been placing prepositions at the end of sentences for centuries, for the very good reason that this is often the best place for them! It is sometimes ▶

possible to reword a sentence so that the preposition does not
fall at the end:

These are the shipping lists you asked for.

↓

These are the shipping lists for which you asked.

But this revised version is more formal and, many would think,
a bit pompous. Often such revisions are impossible. For
example:

Another defeat this weekend doesn't bear thinking about.

So this is one 'rule' that can safely be ignored.

prepositional phrase

A phrase with a PREPOSITION as its HEADWORD. The preposition
comes at the beginning of the phrase and is followed by:

■ a NOUN:

PREPOSITION	NOUN
below	ground

■ a PRONOUN:

PREPOSITION	PRONOUN
after	me

■ a VERBAL NOUN:

PREPOSITION	VERBAL NOUN
without	leaving

■ a NOUN PHRASE:

PREPOSITION	NOUN PHRASE
during	the last month

P

Uses

Prepositional phrases have two main uses:

■ To MODIFY a noun. When they form part of a NOUN PHRASE they normally come after the noun. (So they are, technically, 'postmodifiers'.) For example:

| Court actions **in foreign countries** | expose a company to a |
| noun phrase | number of risks. |

■ As an ADVERBIAL. When they are used as adverbials, they give information about:

    PLACE
    TIME
    MANNER
    REASON
    PURPOSE

prepositional verb

A VERB that is followed by a PREPOSITION. Examples are:

We **decided on** the ballet.

Money worries and overwork **led to** illness.

Prepositional verbs may seem similar to PHRASAL VERBS like *dig up*, but there is a difference in the way they are constructed and used:

	PREPOSITIONAL VERBS	PHRASAL VERBS
Structure Use 1	verb + preposition TRANSITIVE (**must** be followed by an object)	verb + adverb TRANSITIVE or INTRANSITIVE (doesn't have to be followed by an object).
Use 2	Sentence cannot be rearranged. We can only say *We **decided on** the ballet.* We cannot say *We **decided** the ballet **on**.*	Sentence can be rearranged. We can say *They've **dug up** a lot of human bones at my old uncle's house.* We can also say *They've **dug** a lot of human bones **up** at my old uncle's house.*

Some people group prepositional verbs with phrasal verbs. The grammatical distinction described above still, of course, applies.

present continuous tense

A tense that is made by using the PRESENT TENSE of the verb *be* with the PRESENT PARTICIPLE of the MAIN VERB:

VERB STEM	PRESENT CONTINUOUS TENSE:
sing	I am singing, she is singing, you are singing, etc.
be	I am being, she is being, etc.

Uses

The commonest uses of this tense are:

■ actions going on now:

'I **am speaking** from the home of Mrs Browning,' I said.

■ actions continuing over a period including the present:

They **are staying** in a hotel in Durham.

■ actions planned for the future:

Tomorrow we **are holding** a party in our bungalow.

present participle

A form of the VERB. It is made by adding *-ing* to the verb STEM. (If a verb stem ends in 'e', that letter is usually removed.)

VERB STEM	PRESENT PARTICIPLE
sing	singing
write	writing

Uses

■ To form CONTINUOUS TENSES:

	SING	WRITE
PRESENT CONTINUOUS	they are **singing**	they are **writing**
PAST CONTINUOUS	they were **singing**	they were **writing**
	... and so on ...	

■ In NON-FINITE CLAUSES. These are similar in structure and usage to FINITE CLAUSES but they contain no FINITE VERB. Often, too, the subject of the clause is missed out. For example:

| The men | **working** with him | then walked out. |
| | non-finite clause | |

The words *working with him* are a short form for *who were working with him*.

present perfect continuous tense

A tense formed by combining the present perfect of the verb *be* with the PRESENT PARTICIPLE of the MAIN VERB:

SUBJECT	PRESENT PERFECT OF 'BE'	PRESENT PARTICIPLE OF MAIN VERB
she	has been	working
they	have been	writing

Uses

To refer to a repeated or continuous action with effects in the present:

She **has been working** out in Sierra Leone for a number of years.

To refer to a fairly recent activity that was repeated or continuous and is relevant now:

Recently Julia **has been encountering** difficulties.

To explain something in the present by referring to a past action or event:

I'm happy with my decision to rest him because he **has been competing** since January.

present perfect tense

A verb tense formed by combining the present tense of the verb *have* with the past participle of the main verb:

SUBJECT	PRESENT TENSE OF 'HAVE'	PAST PARTICIPLE OF MAIN VERB
she	has	worked
they	have	written

Uses

To describe an incomplete action or series of actions continuing into the present:

> Engel is German by birth but **has lived** in Britain for the last twenty years.

To describe a past action with results continuing to the present:

> Fire **has damaged** a disused hotel at Abingdon.

In an adverbial clause of time referring to the future:

> Massive stars will collapse in on themselves when they **have exhausted** their nuclear fuel.

present tense

One of the two FINITE forms of the verb:

SUBJECT	BE	HAVE	WORK
I	am	have	work
you	are	have	work
he, she, it	is	has	works
we	are	have	work
you	are	have	work
they	are	have	work

In all verbs except *be*, there are two forms. One is the same as the verb stem and is used for all PERSONS except the third person singular (*he, she, it*). The other is the verb stem plus 's', except for verbs that end with a vowel, like *go* where the 's' is preceded by an 'e': *go* → *goes*. In the case of *have*, instead of *haves*, we say *has*.

This tense is also called the SIMPLE PRESENT TENSE, and in this book its uses are listed under that heading.

primary auxiliary verbs

The verbs *be*, *do*, and *have*. Auxiliary verbs are used with a MAIN VERB to form the VERB PHRASE:

SUBJECT	AUXILIARY VERB(S)	MAIN VERB
we	were	walking
he	had	wanted
you	did	know

Be, *do*, and *have* are different from other auxiliary verbs because they can also be used as main verbs. For example:

In England our weather **is** always abnormal.

He **has** a plan.

I **did** a lot of work with business plans.

pronoun

A class of words that 'stand in' for other words, usually:

- nouns
- noun phrases
- other pronouns

Pronouns enable the writer and speaker to avoid long-winded repetitions of things that have already been expressed. (See PRONOUNS IN USE.)

Pronouns fall into seven groups:

Personal

The personal pronouns are:

I/me, we/us, you, he/him, she/her, it, they/them

They are used to refer back to nouns which have already been used in the text:

Machiavelli set out on 17 December 1507. **He** travelled across Lombardy.

Possessive

The possessive pronouns are:

mine, ours, yours, his, hers, its, theirs

They are used in sentences such as:

My cooking's probably even worse than **yours**.

Michael Joseph says there has been no breach: 'The Sunday Times's promotion is **theirs**, not **ours**.'

These are true pronouns because they stand alone, without being attached to a noun, by contrast with *my*, *our*, etc. which always come before a noun and are better referred to as POSSESSIVE DETERMINERS.

Reflexive

These are:

myself, ourselves, yourself, yourselves, himself, herself, itself, themselves

They are used in sentences such as:

'Make **yourselves** comfortable here,' he snapped.

As we tried to calm **ourselves** with sweet coffee, a Swiss traveller appeared.

Demonstrative

The demonstrative pronouns are:

this, that, these, those

When these words stand alone, they are pronouns; for example, in sentences like this:

The strong — **those** in powerful Unions — gained at the expense of the weak.

They can also be used before a noun, in which case they are not pronouns but DETERMINERS:

This decision will cause greater uncertainty.

Interrogative

These are:

who, whom, whose, what, which

They are used in the formation of questions:

What is homeopathy?

Relative

The relative pronouns are:

who, whom, whose, that, which

They are used to introduce RELATIVE CLAUSES:

The artist **who** did my album cover used an airbrush and I got him to do three guitars for me.

Indefinite

This is a large group of pronouns which refer less precisely than the others listed above. They include:

some	someone	somebody	something
any	anyone	anybody	anything
none	no one	nobody	nothing
everyone	everybody	everything	all
either	neither	both	each

For example:

As I keep saying, I don't need you or **anybody** else to tell me what I can or cannot do.

He could hear **nothing**.

---

pronouns in use

In good writing pronouns are used accurately and clearly. In the extract that follows, the pronouns have been highlighted and numbered:

I (1) was met by a minder from the news department, Ian Whitehead, **who** (2) took **me** (3) aside, as **he** (4) was no doubt used to doing with journalists, and told **me** (5) to 'go easy' on His Lordship, **whose** (6) knowledge of Indo-China was limited. With a film camera turning, I (7) began by asking the minister **who** (8) exactly these reasonable Khmer Rouge were. 'Um ... ' **he** (9) replied. When I (10) asked for their names, Whitehead threw **himself** (11) in front of the camera, yelling, 'Stop **this** (12) now! **This** (13) is not the way **we** (14) were led to believe the line of ▶

questioning would go!' No 'line' had been agreed.
Nevertheless, **he** (15) refused to allow the interview to
proceed until **he** (16) had approved the questions.

	WORD	TYPE OF PRONOUN	REFERS TO
1	I	personal	the writer
2	who	relative	a minder from the news department, Ian Whitehead
3	me	personal (objective)	the writer
4	he	personal	Ian Whitehead
5	me	personal (objective)	the writer
6	whose	relative	His Lordship
7	I	personal	the writer
8	who	interrogative	these reasonable Khmer Rouge
9	he	personal	the minister
10	I	personal	the writer
11	himself	reflexive	Whitehead
12	this	demonstrative	the journalist's behaviour
13	this	demonstrative	the line of questioning being pursued
14	we	personal	officials at the Foreign Office
15	he	personal	Whitehead
16	he	personal	Whitehead

As the example shows, pronouns do not always refer to
specific words or phrases in the text. Sometimes they refer to
broader ideas contained in it. For example the writer quotes
Whitehead using *this* twice to refer to the way in which the
minister was being questioned and *we* to refer to him and his
(unnamed) colleagues.

proper noun

A group of words that refer to people, places, and things that are unique. In written English they are spelled with an initial CAPITAL LETTER:

Botswana   Harry

You could object that there is more than one *Harry* in the world, but in speech and writing when we use the word *Harry* it always refers to a unique individual.

Proper nouns can also consist of more than one word:

The Oxford Dictionary of English   The Houses of Parliament

purpose

ADVERBIALS and ADVERBIAL CLAUSES can be used to provide information about **why** things occur — for what purpose they are done.

Adverbials

The commonest type of adverbial used to show purpose is a PREPOSITIONAL PHRASE beginning with *for*:

I've always grown vegetables **for pleasure or necessity**.

Adverbial clauses

Adverbial clauses of purpose often begin with *so that*:

She sat forward **so that she could see into the car's wing mirror**.

Infinitive clauses are also frequently used for this purpose, introduced by *in order to, so as to,* or just *to*:

Someone may grab your collar with both hands **in order to headbutt you in the face**.

In the example above *in order to* could be replaced by either *so as to* or *to*.

question

There are three main types of question in English:

Yes/no question

These expect the answer *yes* or *no* (or possibly *I don't know*):

Are they good jobs?

Did he know just how deeply his father was opposed to things?

Either/or question

A variant on the yes/no question is one which offers a choice of response:

Do you want a strong cup or a weak one?

Here the respondent can't answer *yes* or *no*; the only possible answers are *a strong cup* or *a weak one*.

Question-word question

These are sometimes described as 'open' questions, because they allow the respondent a freer choice of answer. They begin with one of these words:

who(m)   which   what   when   where   why   how

For example:

Why are you doing this?

Who has the papers?

Not all questions fall into one of these three groups. Sometimes a question is asked using a regular statement pattern:

You have the papers?

We indicate to a reader that it is a question by placing a QUESTION MARK at the end of the sentence. In speech the voice is raised at the end of the sentence, rather than falling as it does at the end of a statement.

question mark

This punctuation mark is used to mark the end of a question. It can also be used to indicate that the writer believes that a statement is doubtful or questionable:

Who is Sylvia?

All was going well until a passing lad with a sense of fun (?) pulled out the plug.

quite

This ADVERB has a number of uses, and one of the commonest is as a MODIFIER before an ADJECTIVE or ADVERB. For example:

It is **quite** impossible.

This could happen **quite** rapidly.

As these two examples show, *quite* has two distinct meanings:

■ 'completely': *quite impossible*.

■ 'fairly': *quite rapidly*.

In the following example, the word is used twice, illustrating both meanings:

The defendant stared at her and then **quite** deliberately drove over her, **quite** slowly.

It is important to avoid confusion between the two meanings:

At sixteen Sarah was **quite** beautiful, but she didn't make the most of herself.

Does the writer mean that she was 'very beautiful' or 'fairly beautiful'? It isn't clear.

quotation marks

See INVERTED COMMAS.

reason

ADVERBIALS and ADVERBIAL CLAUSES can be used to answer the question *Why?* to provide information about the reason for something happening.

Adverbials

These are often introduced by expressions such as *because of* and *on account of*:

Did the person leave **because of a management failure**?

Adverbial clauses

These are commonly introduced by the conjunctions *because*, *since*, and *as*:

> Hindley and Catherine were angry **because they had not received any presents**.

> It was not difficult for Anne **since she had been encouraged by her father to practise her clog dancing on the kitchen hearth**.

NON-FINITE CLAUSES are constructed using the PRESENT PARTICIPLE:

> I knew about them **because of being at art college**.

---

reference

reference

We normally read texts in sequence from beginning to end. (Certain texts, like newspapers and magazines, are more likely to be dipped into and not read in the order in which they are printed. But even with these we usually read individual stories or articles from beginning to end.) Good writers make things easier for their readers by referring back to things that have already been mentioned and forwards to things that will be mentioned later. This gives a text COHESION.

There are three main types of reference:

■ REFERRING WORDS: words like pronouns which help us to refer clearly and briefly to what has gone before, or what is coming after, without unnecessary repetition.

■ ELLIPSIS: these are constructions that enable us to refer back to earlier material while missing out sections of sentences (but without confusing the reader).

■ CONJUNCTS and DISJUNCTS: these are ADVERBIALS which help to make the links between sentences clear.

All these are illustrated in BUILDING A TEXT.

referring words

The main types of referring words are:

■ PRONOUNS:

personal (*I*, *she*, etc.).
demonstrative (*this*, *those*, etc.).
relative (*who(m)*, *which*, etc.).

■ DETERMINERS. For example:

All three came from the Midlands and had been at the sharp
end of the business as salesmen for distribution companies.

■ other words and phrases. For example:

former   latter   above   below

regular verb

A verb that follows the following pattern:

	PRESENT TENSE	PAST TENSE	PAST PARTICIPLE
stem	stem (+ -s)	stem + -ed (or + -d, if stem ends with 'e')	stem + -ed (or + -d, if stem ends with 'e')
walk	I walk / she walks	walked	walked

See also IRREGULAR VERB.

r

relative clause

Relative clauses are SUBORDINATE CLAUSES that do a similar job to
adjectives:

She was a **wicked** woman. (adjective)

While they were eating, a woman **who had a bad name** crept
into the room and knelt at the feet of Jesus. (relative clause)

Relative clauses are used as postmodifiers in noun phrases and are
introduced by one of the RELATIVE PRONOUNS:

who, whom, whose, which, that

Sometimes the relative pronoun is missed out:

> Could you be the person **they're looking for**?

This could also be written:

> Could you be the person **whom they're looking for**?

In their full form relative clauses are like mini-sentences. You can remove them from the sentence they are in and, with very few changes, turn them into sentences in their own right:

ORIGINAL	TWO-SENTENCE VERSION
While they were eating, a woman who had a bad name crept into the room and knelt at the feet of Jesus.	While they were eating, a woman crept into the room and knelt at the feet of Jesus. She had a bad name.

It is also possible to have relative clauses that do not contain a finite verb. The verb in a non-finite relative clause can be an infinitive, a present participle, or a past participle:

VERB FORM	SAMPLE SENTENCE	EQUIVALENT USING FINITE VERB
infinitive	That's the way to say it.	That's the way that you should say it.
present participle	The woman talking has raised a large family.	The woman who is talking has raised a large family.
past participle	That's a picture taken from a helicopter or an aeroplane.	That's a picture that was taken from a helicopter or an aeroplane.

r

relative clauses in use

Relative clauses add information to the noun or pronoun they modify. Sometimes that information is essential; without it the sentence would not make much sense:

WITH RELATIVE CLAUSE	WITHOUT RELATIVE CLAUSE
A person who is mentally handicapped is just as much a member of society as anyone else.	A person is just as much a member of society as anyone else.

Removing the relative clause makes a nonsense of the sentence, because we do not know which person is being described. Essential relative clauses of this type are called **defining** relative clauses.

Other relative clauses are not essential to the sentence as a whole; they may add interesting information, but if they are removed the sentence still stands:

WITH RELATIVE CLAUSE	WITHOUT RELATIVE CLAUSE
The minister, who had red hair and fire in his eye, started on an upbeat note.	The minister started on an upbeat note.

Here the information is interesting, but even when the clause is removed, we still know to whom the sentence refers. Clauses of this kind are called **non-defining** relative clauses.

Who(m) or that?

When the relative clause refers to a person it can be introduced by *who*, *whom*, *whose*, or *that*. In standard English any of these pronouns can be used to introduce a defining relative clause, but *that* cannot be used to introduce a non-defining one.

▶

Which or that?

Either of these can introduce a defining relative clause referring to anything non-human, but only *which* can introduce a non-defining one.

No relative pronoun?

When the relative pronoun is the OBJECT of a defining relative clause, the relative pronoun (*whom, which*, or *that*) is often missed out:

> But a woman in black was the only person I saw.

instead of

> But a woman in black was the only person that I saw.

Punctuation

In written English the difference between defining and non-defining relative clauses is marked by punctuation.
Non-defining relative clauses are enclosed by commas:

> The minister, **who had red hair and fire in his eye**, started on an upbeat note.

Do not put commas around a defining relative clause:

> The girl **who had just walked in** was wearing a silver miniskirt.

reported speech

In reports and stories it is often necessary to tell the reader what someone has said. If the words are quoted exactly as spoken, it is DIRECT SPEECH. In writing this is shown by the use of punctuation. In reported speech the actual words are not quoted, but are usually summed up. For example:

1. Both students and lecturers said that they felt that lectures gave an opportunity for personal contact.

2. PC Clifford would have welcomed the tea, but said that he must get back to the scene of the tragedy.

These two examples show two different forms of reported speech.

Generalizing and summarizing

In (1) the writer has summed up what was said. Presumably a number of different people said different things, but all in all they agreed that lectures gave an opportunity for personal contact. Sometimes a writer summarizes even more briefly:

He expressed his concern for the workforce and their families.

Reporting the words

In example (2) the writer is clearly much closer to the actual words used. The police officer probably said something like, '*I must get back to the scene of the tragedy*', although he may not have used those exact words. The extensive quotation of actual words is comparatively rare in reported speech; generalizing and summarizing are much more common.

Verb tense

Stories and reports are normally written using past tenses. This means that the words of reported speech should also be put in the past tense. If someone says, '*I am going to work*', it is reported as *He said that he was going to work*. What happens is that each verb is shifted back in time:

go	becomes	went
is		was
will		would

and so on.

Similarly time adverbials have to be changed:

now	becomes	then
today		that day
yesterday		the day before

and so on.

Personal pronouns, too, have to shift from first person to third:

I	becomes	he/she
us		them

and so on.

So for example:

'At the moment I'm staying with a friend in Peckham,' he said, 'but next week I shall be moving into my own flat.'

becomes

He said that at the time **he was staying** with a friend in Peckham, but that **the following week he would be moving into his** own flat.

result

ADVERBIAL CLAUSES can be used to show the result of an action or situation described in the MAIN CLAUSE:

My father threatened to punish them, **so they were forced to accept my company**. (Action)

The two metal coffee jugs were **so hot that Cormack dropped them with a yelp**. (Situation)

Result clauses can be introduced by:

so	and so	so that
so ... that	such (a) ... that	in such a way that

root

What is left when you remove all prefixes and suffixes from a word:

WORD	PREFIXES AND SUFFIXES	ROOT
misunderstanding	mis-, –under-, -ing	stand
inspirational	in-, -ation-, -al	spir

Sometimes the root may be a word in its own right, like *stand*, but often, like *spir*, it is not. (But the root *spir*, which is Latin in origin, occurs in other words such as *aspired, transpiration*, and *expire*.)

second person

You. It is a category used in classifying verbs and personal pronouns that are referring to a person being addressed.

semicolon

Semicolons are used to mark a break between two parts of a sentence. Usually the two parts that are separated in this way are FINITE CLAUSES, which could stand as sentences in their own right. You use a semicolon because you want to show that there is a close link between them:

> He loved chasing women, but did not like them; it was the chase that excited him.

If you write this as two separate sentences, you change the meaning slightly by increasing the separation between the two ideas:

> He loved chasing women, but did not like them. It was the chase that excited him.

Some writers try to use a comma instead of a semicolon for this purpose. This is a mistake. The comma is weaker and when we are reading it does not 'stop' the eye in the same way as a semicolon:

> He loved chasing women, but did not like them, it was the chase that excited him.

The 'comma splice', as this is called, is best avoided.

Lists

If a list contains items that are quite long, semicolons can be used instead of commas to separate them:

> Weeds may reach the lawn in various ways: as seeds blown by the wind; carried by birds; brought in on muddy footwear, machinery, or tools; or concealed in unsterilized soil or badly made compost used for top dressing.

See also COMMAS, COLONS, AND SEMICOLONS.

sentence

A unit of language consisting of one or more FINITE CLAUSES. If a sentence contains just one clause, it is described as SIMPLE:

> The commissioners entered Pisa on Friday 8 June.

> Surrounded by high waves, in the middle of the North Sea, a team of French engineers are constructing the first offshore oil-rig platforms.

As the second of the examples shows, simple sentences are not necessarily either short or simple in meaning.

If a sentence contains more than one finite clause it is described as multiple. In the example that follows the clauses are marked:

Nobody is sure	whether it will work	but everything has to be done fast.

Multiple sentences can be either COMPOUND or COMPLEX.

sentence adverbial

CONJUNCTS and DISJUNCTS are described as sentence adverbials. They are used in a piece of continuous writing to link different parts together. They work in a variety of ways, including:

Adding and listing

In narratives, explanations, and arguments we often want to place items in a particular order. We indicate this fact and show the order by using words like 'firstly':

> **Firstly**, the feeling for the tradition is very strong in the village; **secondly**, Gawthorpe is an ancient settlement — its history can be traced back to a Viking chief named Gorky and there is evidence that it existed in Roman times; **thirdly**, the original custom was to bring in a new May tree each year.

Sometimes the sequence is less important, but we still wish to make it clear that items are linked:

> Cynics may scoff that he is yet another stiff-upper-lip, old-soldier type, having come like so many of the august men of the Club from a military background before moving on to the sugar industry. And, as he admitted yesterday, he has little knowledge of the racing industry, apart from having been 'a very amateur rider'. **Furthermore**, the fact that Haines must report to the Jockey Club Stewards and has no authority to act unilaterally has inevitably led to suggestions that his is merely a token appointment.

Sentence adverbials used in this way include:

also	as well	at the same time	besides
finally	first	furthermore	in addition
last	meanwhile	moreover	next
soon	then	too	

Giving examples

Sometimes we wish to introduce an example or a list of material which exemplifies part of the argument:

> These birds are not evenly distributed along the coast. **For example**, scoter are mainly confined to East Sussex and mergansers to West Sussex ...

Other words used in this way are:

. namely   as follows

Saying things another way

We may also wish to restate something using different words:

> Pagan festivals were incorporated into the church calendar, fertility rites becoming Christian processions. The yule log became a Christmas 'ingredient'; many magic springs became holy wells, still capable of healing the sick. **In other words,** the church controlled popular magic by offering its own brand.

Cause and result

In texts that contain an argument one sentence is often the logical development of what has gone before:

> The nation's filmmakers, like its people, can't express emotion; they lack drive and passion, they're tame and repressed. **As a result**, the British can write novels and plays, even produce an occasional world-class painter but, when it comes to cinema, they might as well forget it.

Other sentence adverbials of this type are:

| accordingly | as a result | consequently | hence |
| so | therefore | thus | |

Contrasts and alternatives

A sentence can be contrasted with what has gone before:

> The speed of sound in water is roughly four times as great as it is in air. **On the other hand**, water is not much different for taste and smell, and much worse for vision.

Other sentence adverbials of this type are:

all the same	alternatively	anyway	by contrast
conversely	even so	however	instead
nevertheless	on the other hand	rather	yet

Concession

Another type of contrast is similar to that used in adverbial clauses of concession: despite this fact, the following is true. For example:

> Anyone could have attacked Ella. Why should it be the O'Neills just because Ella had tried to befriend Kathleen? **Nevertheless**, she felt uneasy and was almost glad to hear that a second girl had been attacked in a different part of Liverpool.

Other sentence adverbials of this type are:

however	yet	even so

shall

A MODAL AUXILIARY VERB used in the formation of FUTURE TENSES:

SIMPLE FUTURE	I/we shall see
FUTURE CONTINUOUS	I/we shall be seeing
FUTURE PERFECT	I/we shall have seen
FUTURE PERFECT CONTINUOUS	I/we shall have been seeing

As these examples demonstrate, *shall* is traditionally used for the FIRST PERSON (*I* and *we*). But *will* is frequently instead of *shall*: see WILL/SHALL.

S

should

A MODAL AUXILIARY VERB used to refer to possible events in the future:

> I should be there before then.

It is also used to express how desirable something is:

> He said that they should see a speech therapist.

simple aspect

In the verb system of English, verbs can refer to the PRESENT, the PAST, or the FUTURE. Within each of these 'time zones' we can make the VERB PHRASE provide information about the duration and/or completeness of an action. This is called the verb 'aspect'.

The simple aspect is, as the name suggests, the one that provides least additional information. The continuous aspect lays stress on something going on over a period of time:

> They are staying at a hotel in Durham.

The perfect aspect often suggests that an action is complete but still has some relevance to the present time:

> Sawyer has written to the SSI to complain.

The simple aspect does neither of these. More information about how it works is given in these entries: SIMPLE FUTURE TENSE, SIMPLE PAST TENSE, and SIMPLE PRESENT TENSE.

simple future tense

A tense formed by using the MODAL AUXILIARY VERBS *will* or *shall* followed by the VERB STEM:

> You will tell.

Uses

Prediction:

> Over the coming weeks councillors **will attempt** to cover the £200,000 loss.

Indicating determination or commitment:

> The Labour Government **will** immediately **make** available £1bn to invest in the NHS.

To show ability:

> A pair of kitchen scales **will do** that easily.

To describe habits:

> Feminists **will keep on** about language.

simple past tense

A tense used to refer to actions in the past. In REGULAR VERBS it is formed by adding -ed to the verb stem (or just -d if the verb stem ends in e):

> You walked.

Uses

To refer to a single action in the past:

> On 25 May 1812 the Felling pit in Durham **exploded**, killing 92 men and boys.

To refer to a regular or repeated action in the past:

> They **met** several times last week.

> The mobile shop **called** once a week.

simple present tense

A tense formed by using the VERB STEM, which is followed by 's' in the third person singular:

	SINGULAR	PLURAL
1ST PERSON	I walk	we walk
2ND PERSON	you walk	you walk
3RD PERSON	he/she/it walks	they walk

Uses

■ present feelings and thoughts:

> 'I **feel** rather sick,' she said.

- actions or states that are true *now* but have no particular reference to time:

    He **lives** in London.

- timeless truths:

    Fairly pure water **freezes** at about 0°C.

- habitual actions:

    Nearly a quarter of men **clean out** their cars once a month.

- open CONDITIONALS:

    If I **see** anything wrong, I'll **ring** you later from my surgery.

- scheduled future actions:

    The following day, we **travel** to Berlin.

- newspaper headlines:

    Ministers **flout** arms sales code

- informal narrative:

    And he **says** to her, 'What did you do before you joined the police?'

- retelling a story in, for example, a review:

    Enter the Hero, who then **fights** it **out** with the baddies.

- in sports commentaries:

    In it **goes**, but it**'s** too strong for Hasselbaink.

simple sentence

A sentence that consists of one FINITE CLAUSE. Examples are:

    The commissioners entered Pisa on Friday 8 June.

    Surrounded by high waves, in the middle of the North Sea, a team of French engineers are constructing the first offshore oil-rig platforms.

As the second of the examples shows, simple sentences are not necessarily either short or simple in meaning.

since

Conjunction

A SUBORDINATING CONJUNCTION used to introduce two types of adverbial clause:

■ time:

> **Since** we moved here the asthma has got worse.

■ reason:

> The Germans thought Danzig might be bombed but not Gdynia, **since** the latter is a Polish city.

Preposition

It is also used as a preposition:

> I haven't seen her **since** Monday.

singular

One of the two NUMBERS in English, singular and PLURAL. NOUNS, PRONOUNS, and VERBS can change according to whether they are singular or plural.

slang

Words and expressions that are informal and not STANDARD ENGLISH. Different social groups often use a special vocabulary. Sometimes this is fairly widespread and well understood. In the sentences that follow the slang expressions are in bold type.

> If Martin is prepared to take the risk, he could be **quids in**.

> I just wanted to be sure you weren't trying **to pull a fast one** on me.

> I'm a bit **skint** at the moment.

Some slang is confined to small tightly knit groups who can use it to exclude outsiders. Slang is also often sexual or scatological.

slash

A punctuation mark with these uses:

■ to indicate alternatives:

A trainee can amass as many credits as **he/she** likes.

■ to show a range:

Accounts for the year **1999/2000**

■ in some abbreviations:

c/o

split infinitive

The infinitive is the form of the verb made by adding *to* to its
STEM:

to go

Some traditionalists say that you should never place anything
between the *to* and the stem. They argue that since the
infinitive is a part of the verb it should never be split. So it is
wrong to say *to boldly go*. You should instead say *to go boldly* or
boldly to go.

There is no grammatical justification for this so-called 'rule',
and people have been splitting infinitives for centuries.
Indeed sometimes it is impossible to convey your meaning
unless you do split an infinitive. For example:

Everyone else thought they were too young **to really cope**
with adult responsibilities.

If you move *really* to another position you change the
meaning of the sentence:

Everyone else thought they were too young **really to cope**
with adult responsibilities.

Everyone else thought they were too young **to cope really**
with adult responsibilities.

S

standard English

The form of English that is most widely understood across the country. In different regions and social classes different DIALECTS may be used. This means that it is sometimes difficult for a person from one region to understand what is being said by a person from another; a Cornish person, for example, may struggle to understand what is said by someone from Liverpool or Newcastle. This is not just a matter of accent; each dialect has its own distinctive vocabulary and variations of grammar. The problem can be overcome if both speakers can also use standard English. This is the version of English which is described by grammars and other books about language. Expressions and constructions that differ from it are described as 'non-standard'.

stem

The base form of the verb. In regular verbs all the other forms of the verb are constructed using the stem:

STEM	walk
INFINITIVE	to walk
PRESENT TENSE	walk/walks
PRESENT PARTICIPLE	walking
PAST TENSE	walked
PAST PARTICIPLE	walked

structure word

The vocabulary of English can be divided into CONTENT WORDS and structure words. Structure words are:

- CONJUNCTIONS
- PREPOSITIONS
- PRONOUNS
- DETERMINERS

S

subject

In a statement clause, the subject:

■ comes at or near the beginning of the clause

■ comes before the verb

■ agrees with the verb in number and person

■ often denotes the doer of an action.

It also often gives a clear idea of what the sentence is about.

The subject can be:

■ a noun:

Yoga is religious.

■ a verbal noun:

Dancing is a wonderful way of keeping in training.

■ an infinitive:

To err is human.

■ a pronoun:

They argued ferociously about Ireland.

■ a noun phrase:

The core of the problem is simple.

■ a noun clause:

What he said was true.

subject complement

Part of a CLAUSE that completes the subject. In a statement clause it comes after the verb and refers to the same person, thing, or idea as the subject. For example:

SUBJECT	VERB	SUBJECT COMPLEMENT
My job	is	very unusual.
Alton man Giles Stogdon	will become	the new police chief for Winchester.

The verb in sentences like this works in a similar way to an equal sign:

| My job | = | very unusual. |

A subject complement can be:

■ a noun:

> Cash is **king**.

■ a pronoun:

> It was **you**!

■ a numeral:

> I was **third**.

■ a noun phrase:

> Alton man Giles Stogdon will become **the new police chief for Winchester**.

■ an adjective or adjective phrase:

> My job is **very unusual**.

subordinate clause

In a complex sentence there is one MAIN CLAUSE and one (or more) clauses that depend on it. If you break the sentence into its separate clauses you usually find that the main clause will still stand up if you replace the other clause(s) with a single word:

	MAIN CLAUSE	SUBORDINATE CLAUSE
COMPLEX SENTENCE	The problem is	that Israel wants to choose both teams on the football pitch.
SIMPLE SENTENCE	The problem is this.	

The main clause can follow one of the seven standard patterns (see CLAUSE). Within the structure of the main clause, subordinate clauses can act as:

■ SUBJECT:

> **What I want to do now** is to look at two elements.

■ OBJECT:

> Describe how **the accident happened**.

■ SUBJECT COMPLEMENT:

> The problem is **that Israel wants to choose both teams on the football pitch**.

■ OBJECT COMPLEMENT:

> They had made him **what he was**.

■ ADVERBIAL:

> We'll talk about it **when we meet this evening**.

In each case the subordinate clause can be replaced by a single word or a short phrase, without changing the grammar of the main clause:

> **My aim** is to look at two elements.

> Describe **the accident**.

> The problem is **this**.

> They had made him **that**.

> We'll talk about it **later**.

subordinating conjunction

A conjunction used to introduce a SUBORDINATE CLAUSE. Examples are:

when	how	where	why
if	although	unless	since
because	until	so	as

suffix

Part of a word that comes after the BASE. In the list of words that follows, the suffixes are printed in bold type:

> child**ish**　king**dom**　pictur**esque**

Suffixes make a new word out of the base. They often also change it from one WORD CLASS to another. So, for example, the NOUN *child* becomes the ADJECTIVE *childish*.

suffixes in use

Verb suffixes

SUFFIX	EXAMPLE	FROM
-ify	beautify	beauty
-ize/-ise	idolize	idol

Adjective suffixes

SUFFIX	EXAMPLE	FROM
-able/-ible	excitable	excite
-al/-ial	adverbial	adverb
-ate	sensate	sense
-ed	flat-roofed	flat roof
-esque	picturesque	picture
-ful	fateful	fate
-ic	Icelandic	Iceland
-ical	economical	economy
-ish	childish	child
-ive	plaintive	plaint
-less	childless	child
-like	doglike	dog
-ous	analogous	analogy
-y	dozy	doze

Adverb suffixes

SUFFIX	EXAMPLE	FROM
-ly	happily	happy
-ward(s)	westwards	west
-wise	clockwise	clock

S

Noun suffixes

SUFFIX	EXAMPLE	FROM
-age	acreage	acre
-al	referral	refer
-ant/-ent	inhabitant	inhabit
-ation/-ion	examination	examine
-dom	kingdom	king
-ee	addressee	address
-eer	auctioneer	auction
-er	abstainer	abstain
-ery	effrontery	front
-ess	tigress	tiger
-ette	leatherette	leather
-ful	handful	hand
-hood	neighbourhood	neighbour
-ing	mooring	moor
-ism	impressionism	impression
-ist	pianist	piano
-ity	chastity	chaste
-ment	postponement	postpone
-ness	happiness	happy
-ocracy	meritocracy	merit
-or	director	direct
-ship	directorship	director
-ster	trickster	trick

superlative

Many adjectives can have three forms:

ABSOLUTE	COMPARATIVE	SUPERLATIVE
small	smaller	smallest
attractive	more attractive	most attractive

The COMPARATIVE form is used when comparing two items; the superlative is used when there are more than two:

> She is **smaller** than her brother. (**comparative**)

The **smallest** of the three specialist colleges, it has just over 150 full-time students, of whom about half come from Wales. (**superlative**)

The superlative is formed in different ways according to the length of the base adjective. If it has one syllable, then the letters -*est* are added. If the word has three syllables or more then the word *most* is placed before the adjective: *most attractive*. Words of two syllables vary: some add -*est* and some use *most*. Some even do either, for example *clever*.

Spelling: adding -est

■ If the word ends in a consonant, add –*est* (*quick* becomes *quickest*).

■ Words of one syllable with a short vowel sound and ending with a single consonant, double the consonant and add –*est* (*sad* becomes *saddest*).

■ With words of one syllable ending in 'l', you normally do **not** double the 'l', but *cruel* becomes *cruellest*.

■ If it ends in 'e', add –*st* (*late* becomes *latest*).

■ If it ends in 'y', change the 'y' to an 'i' and add –*est* (*happy* becomes *happiest*).

Classifying adjectives

Some adjectives are used to place nouns into groups or categories, for example *nuclear* and *annual*. Adjectives of this type do not have a comparative or superlative form. You cannot talk about a *more nuclear power station* or *the most annual concert*.

syllable

English words consist of one or more syllables. Each syllable always contains one speech VOWEL. This may have one or more speech CONSONANTS before and/or after it. In the examples that follow, the words are broken into syllables:

1 syllable	yacht	house	a
2 syllables	hap-py	lang-uage	prac-tice
3 syllables	bi-cy-cle	sen-si-ble	ac-cid-ent

synonym

A word that has the same or similar meaning to another. The following pairs of words are synonyms:

still	motionless
melody	tune
birth control	contraception
sluggish	lethargic
loud	noisy

See also ANTONYM.

syntax

The study of how words are selected and arranged to form sentences. Syntax is a major part of grammar, the other being MORPHOLOGY.

tag question

A question 'tagged on' to the end of a statement. For example:

Those daffodils have gone pale, **haven't they**?

She shouldn't have left, **should she**?

You thought it was still six, **didn't you**?

When a speaker uses a tag question, he or she normally expects agreement or confirmation from the listener.

Structure

If the statement contains an AUXILIARY VERB the tag question repeats this, as in the first two examples. If the statement verb is in the SIMPLE PRESENT or the SIMPLE PAST then the tag question uses *do* or *did*, as in the last example.

If the speaker expects the answer *Yes*, then the tag question is in the negative (as in the first and last examples). If the answer *No* is expected, then the tag question is in the positive, as in the second example.

Pronunciation

Tag questions can be made confidently. In this case they are spoken with falling intonation. If the speaker is more tentative then they are spoken with a rising tone.

tense

Strictly speaking, in the terminology of modern grammar, English only has two tenses: past and present:

VERB	PRESENT TENSE	PAST TENSE
walk	walk/walks	walked
write	write/writes	wrote

Many people are surprised to be told that English has no future tense — and for everyday purposes it isn't a particularly helpful way of describing how English verbs work. It's more useful to talk about the whole VERB PHRASE and to look at the way it gives information about TIME and ASPECT. If we do this, we can say that English has the following tenses:

	SIMPLE	CONTINUOUS	PERFECT	PERFECT CONTINUOUS
PAST	I walked	I was walking	I had walked	I had been walking
PRESENT	I walk	I am walking	I have walked	I have been walking
FUTURE	I shall/will walk	I shall/will be walking	I shall/will have walked	I shall/will have been walking

tenses in English

Many foreign students of English find the verb system difficult to grasp and even native speakers sometimes make mistakes. This is because the VERB PHRASE in a sentence provides two different types of information:

Time

The verb phrase tells us whether an event happened in the past or present, or is yet to happen in the future.

▶

Aspect

It also provides information about how the speaker regards any action communicated by the verb. Each of the following verb phrases refers to the present:

> I walk (SIMPLE PRESENT)
> I am walking (PRESENT CONTINUOUS)
> I have walked (PRESENT PERFECT)
> I have been walking (PRESENT PERFECT CONTINUOUS)

But it is obvious that they refer to the present in different ways. The SIMPLE PRESENT TENSE has a range of uses which include eternal truths:

> Fairly pure water freezes at about 0° C.

and regular or habitual actions:

> Nearly a quarter of men clean out their cars once a month.

The PRESENT CONTINUOUS TENSE, on the other hand, places more emphasis on an action that continues over a period of time:

> 'I **am speaking** from the home of Mrs Browning,' I said.

If we use the PRESENT PERFECT TENSE, we place yet another emphasis — on the fact that a completed action still has some importance to the present moment:

> But the Government **has said** public money will not be available for at least 15 years.

The Government said it in the past, but this is still important at the time of speaking; in a sense the 'saying' is still going on because the Government has apparently not changed its mind. We can even combine the perfect and continuous aspects:

> Labour's deputy leader **has been saying** to the councils, 'You may not get as much as you want, but you will certainly get more.'

He has said this to the councils over a period of time; it was in the past but is still important at the time of speaking.

This combination of tense and aspect makes it possible to communicate small and subtle differences of meaning.

that

A word with a number of different uses:

■ DEMONSTRATIVE PRONOUN:

I could get on with a man like **that**.

■ DETERMINER:

That book is still funny.

■ RELATIVE PRONOUN:

I stared back blandly with the same expression **that** he was trying on me.

■ SUBORDINATING CONJUNCTION:

A couple of times she had complained **that** he was trying to adopt her.

In uses 3 and 4 the word *that* is often omitted, especially in less formal writing and speaking:

A couple of times she had complained he was trying to adopt her.

that/which/who(m)

These are the three commonest RELATIVE PRONOUNS used to introduce RELATIVE CLAUSES. *Who(m)* is used to refer to people. *That* can be used to refer to people or things, while *which* is only used to refer to things. The main differences between *that* and *which* can be set out like this:

USE	THAT	WHICH
to refer to people	quite common (along *with who(m)*)	almost never
to introduce DEFINING RELATIVE CLAUSES	very common	less common
to introduce NON-DEFINING RELATIVE CLAUSES	almost never	nearly always (in reference to things); when referring to people *who(m)* is used
formal writing	less common	more common
informal writing	more common	less common

See also RELATIVE CLAUSES IN USE.

theirs

A POSSESSIVE PRONOUN. It is sometimes written with an apostrophe (*their's*). This is incorrect.

then

This has three uses:

■ adverb:

I didn't know it **then**, but I know it now.

■ conjunction:

The President spoke and spoke well, **then** sat down.

■ adjective (less common):

The advice on bending the rules came from the **then** Defence Minister, Alan Clark.

third person

He, she, it, and *they*. It is a category used in classifying verbs and personal pronouns that are referring to a third party.

time

We can use adverbials and adverbial clauses to show time.

Adverbials

Adverbials are a common way of indicating when something happened. They may be:

■ ADVERBS:

'How are you feeling?' asked Michael **afterwards**.

Common time adverbs are:

afterwards	already	daily	earlier
ever	finally	first	frequently
hourly	immediately	last	later
monthly	never	next	now
often	presently	seldom	shortly
sometimes	soon	still	suddenly
then	today	tomorrow	usually
weekly	yearly	yesterday	yet

■ ADVERBIAL PHRASES: these are phrases built up on an adverb HEADWORD. For example:

    shortly afterwards   almost daily   much earlier

    Much later I asked, 'Do you still miss Simon a lot?'

■ PREPOSITIONAL PHRASES:

    D. Long will report back **after the Tokyo meeting**.

Prepositional phrases used as time adverbials often begin with:

after	at	before	by	during
for	from	in	on	since
throughout	to	until		

Adverbial clauses

Adverbial clauses of time are introduced by SUBORDINATING CONJUNCTIONS including:

after	as	before	since
until	when	while	

They can be used to describe events that happen:

■ before the event in the main clause:

    When they heard the news they issued statements.

■ at the same time as the event in the main clause:

    While this was being done, Byrne and Phillips went off on a recce down to the road.

■ after the event in the main clause:

    It came out of the blue **before he knew he was famous**.

t

---

time and tense

English has two main ways of showing **when** something happened:

Verb Tense

So, for example, *they will arrive* refers to the future, while *they arrived* refers to the past. ▶

Adverbials and adverbial clauses of time

For example:

yesterday   tomorrow   in two week's time
last year   when they arrive

Often these two work together:

We started the contract   in April of last year.
      ↓   ↓

PAST TENSE   ADVERBIAL

Sometimes, however, tense and time adverbials seem to work against each other. The PRESENT CONTINUOUS TENSE can be combined with adverbials of time to refer to the future as well as the present:

The firm **is working** on that standard now.

Later on in the year she **is travelling** to South Africa to visit her daughter Michelle.

The SIMPLE PRESENT TENSE can be used for an even wider range of times:

I **place** a teabag and some powdered milk into the enamel cup and then **pour** on the water and **stir** with a twig. (present)

Tomorrow night we **travel** to Potosi. (future)

'I want to talk to him,' he **says** to the guard at the door. (past)

My mum and dad **go** there every year. (past, present, and future)

transitive verb

A verb that takes an OBJECT:

SUBJECT	VERB	OBJECT
They	hit	the crossbar.

Some verbs are always or usually transitive. For example:

admire	avoid	buy	complete	cover	create
cut	damage	demand	destroy	discover	enjoy
expect	find	get	give	hit	keep
like	love	make	mean	need	own
prefer	produce	raise	receive	remove	risk
seek	take	use	want	wear	

Other verbs can be both transitive and intransitive (i.e. they do not take an object). An example is the verb *run*:

> He **ran** a successful wine business in Marylebone. (transitive)

> I just left my car and **ran**. (intransitive)

Two objects

Some transitive verbs have two objects, a direct object and an indirect object:

we	gave	them	an early Christmas present
she	told	me	the story
SUBJECT	VERB	INDIRECT OBJECT	DIRECT OBJECT

As the examples show, the two types of object convey a different meaning. The indirect object tells us about the person or thing that benefits from the action described by the verb: *they* received the early Christmas present; *I* heard the story.

Verbs which commonly have an indirect object as well as a direct one include:

bring	buy	give	promise
send	show	teach	tell

uncountable noun

Countable nouns have both a SINGULAR and a PLURAL form. Most nouns are countable, because they refer to things that can be counted. By contrast, a smaller number of nouns do not regularly have a plural form and are called **uncountable**. Examples include:

mud   snow   butter

In addition, many ABSTRACT NOUNS are normally uncountable. For example

unhappiness   dread   darkness

Many uncountable nouns can, however, also be used in the plural in certain circumstances. For example *beer* is usually uncountable, but can be a countable in sentences such as:

beers of the world.

See also COUNTABLE AND UNCOUNTABLE NOUNS.

unique

This word is a classifying ADJECTIVE. Classifying adjectives put things into groups or classes so they cannot normally be MODIFIED by having adverbs such as *very* placed in front of them. *Unique* means 'of which there is only one', so it is, strictly speaking, wrong to say, for example:

He was a very unique person.

And the following example is doubly absurd:

Almost the most unique residential site along the South Coast.

On the other hand there are a small number of modifiers that can be used with *unique*. The most obvious is *almost*:

Britain is **almost unique** in continuing to charge almost all its domestic customers on an unmeasured basis. [for water]

This can be justified because it means that Britain is not the only country to do this; there are a few others.

There is, however, a looser meaning frequently given (especially in informal speech and writing) to *unique*: 'outstanding or remarkable'. When it is used in this sense it is often preceded by *very*:

A **very unique** 'Town' house situated a stone's throw away from the River Thames and Oxford City Centre.

until

A word with two main uses:

Subordinating conjunction

It is used to introduce an ADVERBIAL CLAUSE OF TIME:

It's the kind of thing you don't think of **until** it actually happens to you.

Preposition

It forms PREPOSITIONAL PHRASES used as adverbials of time:

The outside bar provides drinks and snacks **until the early hours of the morning**.

verb

In grammar this word is used in two separate but linked ways:

■ It describes a particular WORD CLASS in the same way that 'noun', 'preposition', and 'adjective' do.

■ It describes a part of a CLAUSE in the same way that 'subject', 'object', and 'complement' do. In this sense it is also sometimes called the VERB PHRASE.

As a word class, verbs are used for three main purposes:

■ to express an action:

She **fled** upstairs to the bathroom.

■ to express a state:

She **slept** noiselessly.

■ to link the SUBJECT with its COMPLEMENT:

She **was** alone.

Verbs can be REGULAR or IRREGULAR and have the following forms:

STEM	walk	swim	be
INFINITIVE	to walk	to swim	to be
PRESENT TENSE	walk/walks	swim/swims	am/is/are
PRESENT PARTICIPLE	walking	swimming	being
PAST TENSE	walked	swam	was/were
PAST PARTICIPLE	walked	swum	been

v

verb phrase

The verb component of a clause. It may consist of one word or several. If it is one word, then that word is a MAIN VERB. If it is more than one word, then one is the MAIN VERB and the others are AUXILIARY VERBS. In statements the verb phrase normally comes after the SUBJECT and before the OBJECT or COMPLEMENT:

SUBJECT	VERB	OBJECT	COMPLEMENT
The music	played.		
It	was		their home.
It	changed	my life.	

The verb phrase in a clause can be FINITE or NON-FINITE and agrees with the subject in NUMBER and PERSON.
See also AGREEMENT.

verbal noun

The PRESENT PARTICIPLE form of the VERB used as a noun. It is also called a 'gerund'. For example:

Smoking is not permitted.

I don't like **eating** a lot late at night.

Although the verbal noun is used as a noun, it also behaves like a verb. The second example can be analysed like this:

SUBJECT	VERB PHRASE	OBJECT	
I	don't like	**eating**	a lot	late at night.
		VERB	OBJECT	ADVERBIAL

Because a verbal noun is partly a noun and partly a verb, it can raise questions when preceded by a noun or pronoun. For example, which of the following sentences is correct?

1. She hates **my** doing that.

2. She hates **me** doing that.

Traditionalists say that (1) is correct and (2) is wrong. In fact 90 per cent of the time people follow the pattern of (2), and the use of a POSSESSIVE before a verbal noun as in (1) is largely confined to fiction and very formal writing.

vocabulary

The words of a language. Linguists sometimes refer to it as 'lexis'. It can be divided into CONTENT WORDS and STRUCTURE WORDS.

voice

English verbs have two voices:

■ active:

I shot the sheriff.

■ passive:

The sheriff was shot by me.

vowel

A word with two meanings:

■ In writing, the five letters *a   e   i   o   u*

■ In speech, sounds made with the mouth open and the airway unobstructed (by contrast with consonants, where the flow of air is briefly obstructed in some way). The exact number of vowels depends on regional accent, but there are more than twenty English vowels.

when

The main uses of *when* are:

■ question word:

When did you last see your father?

■ relative pronoun:

I cannot recall an occasion **when** he asked me for help before.

■ subordinating conjunction introducing a noun clause:

I haven't told them **when** I start.

■ subordinating conjunction introducing an adverbial clause of time:

The off-season hotel had been empty **when** she arrived.

w

where

The main uses of *where* are:

- question word:

  Where shall we go?

- relative pronoun:

  It was not difficult to find the place **where** the prisoners were hiding.

- subordinating conjunction introducing a noun clause:

  Have you told them **where** I live?

- subordinating conjunction introducing an adverbial clause of place:

  Put it **where** it gets as much sun as possible.

while

A SUBORDINATING CONJUNCTION used to introduce ADVERBIAL CLAUSES of TIME:

Sue sat quietly and smiled **while** this was happening.

It also introduces adverbial clauses of CONCESSION:

But **while** this may well provide some help, it will not produce answers.

In the past the form *whilst* was also widely used. This is less common today.

who/whom

Relative clauses can be introduced by these relative pronouns:

who/whom/whose   which   that

The choice between *who* and *whom* can sometimes cause problems. The traditional rules are these:

- Use *who* as the SUBJECT of the VERB:

  Any members **who find** themselves in the Adelaide area can be assured of a warm welcome there.

■ Use *whom* as the OBJECT of the verb:

   The God **whom** we worship.

■ Use *whom* after PREPOSITIONS:

   To **whom** have you complained?

These rules should still be followed in formal writing. Increasingly, however, *who* is replacing *whom* in speech and less formal writing. For example:

   They had to say **who** they supported.

instead of

   They had to say **whom** they supported.

And

   Currently, most people won't go and see a band **who** they haven't heard **of**.

instead of

   Currently, most people won't go and see a band **of whom** they haven't heard.

who's/whose

These two are sometimes confused.

■ *who's* is the short form of *who is*:

   Doctors said last night Watson, 27, **who's** suffering head injuries, was progressing slowly.

■ *whose* is the POSSESSIVE form of *who* and means 'belonging to whom':

   Whose house was it, anyway?

will

A MODAL AUXILIARY VERB used:

■ to refer to possible events in the future:

   At 59, he **will** be the oldest coach in the First Division.

w

■ to ask someone to do something:

> **Will** you take Donald for a little walk, Christine?' her mother asked her when she came home from school one afternoon.

■ to show determination:

> 'He **will** be disciplined,' he said flatly.

■ to volunteer or show willingness:

> He **will** not reveal their names without permission.

■ to describe a person's habits (usually undesirable):

> Your mother **will** do that.

will/shall

The traditional grammar rules are:

■ Use *shall* with *I* and *we*.

■ Use *will* with all other PERSONS.

■ Reverse this for emphasis:

> The sea **shall** not have them.

Increasingly *will* is used across the board. *Shall* is by far the least common MODAL AUXILIARY VERB; in conversation *will* is used fourteen times more frequently than *shall* (despite the frequency that *I* occurs in speech). The only occasion when *shall* is normally used with *I* and *we* is in questions:

> **Shall** I come with you?

Using *will* in such questions is confined to dialect.

word class

A group of words that have the same grammatical function. (In traditional grammar, called a PART OF SPEECH.) Nouns, adjectives, verbs, and adverbs are referred to as open word classes, since their membership is still changing as old words die and new ones are born. Pronouns, prepositions, conjunctions, and determiners (including articles) are closed classes because their membership is fixed.

W

word family

One stem combined with a variety of prefixes and suffixes produces a group of words or a family. Thus the stem *weight* is the parent of this word family:

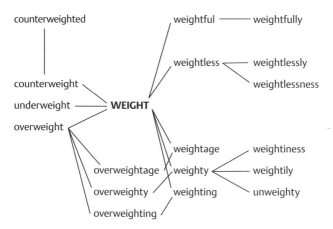

word structure

Words can consist of one or more parts:

PREFIX	STEM	SUFFIX
	weight	
	weight	-less
counter-	weight	
counter-	weight	-ed

The ways in which these parts are combined constitute their structure.

W

would

A MODAL AUXILIARY VERB used to refer to a range of possibilities in the future. For example:

> If Catherine wanted something, I **would** give it to her.

> I think she **would** feel left out.

The effect of using *would* instead of *will* can be seen when we make the substitution:

> If Catherine wants something, I **will** give it to her.

> I think she **will** feel left out.

The versions using *will* are more open: the event may or may not happen. The sentences using *would* seem less open and less likely, although the event is still theoretically possible.

Other uses of *would* are:

- habitual actions in the past:

> Often she **would** go to Nairobi or the coast for a break.

- actions that are regarded as typical:

> He **would** do that, wouldn't he?

Would is often followed by *have*, which turns it into a past tense:

> I don't suppose they **would have** liked it.

In speech this is often shortened to *would've*, which people sometimes confuse with *would of*:

> A number of mourners were quite abusive after the service and if I had not found the funeral so moving I **would of** asked one or two to step into the vestry.

This is, of course, never correct.